Praise for **How to Protect (or Destroy)**

"The tools of online content and social media give everyone who wants one a (potentially loud) public voice. This profound revolution in human communications is terribly exciting, but comes with risks because anyone can say anything at any time, whether true or not. John expertly guides you through the challenges and pitfalls of online reputation so you put your best face forward when customers are looking for you or your brand on the Web."

—David Meerman Scott, best-selling author of
The New Rules of Marketing and PR,
now in 25 languages from Arabic to Vietnamese

"Every day we read about e-mail addresses hacked here or private pictures being posted there, and we never think it will happen to us. The sad truth is that our secrets   financial, medical, personal, and more—are just a click or two away from being stolen and exploited. Instead of being digital ostriches with your head in the sand, the best defense is to read John David's timely book and put his techniques to work protecting your precious digital data. Do it now before it's too late."

—Bruce Turkel, CEO of Turkel Brands and author of
All About Them

"Having known John David as a top public relations consultant for more than 20 years, I can attest to his expertise with complex communications issues. Reading this book, he immerses you in the increasingly complicated world of online reputation, explains our frightening vulnerabilities and artfully describes how we can and should defend ourselves. **How to Protect (or Destroy) Your Reputation Online** is a must-read for CEOs, business owners and students alike."

—Scott Page, CEO of The Lifeline Program and author of
It's Never Too Late

"This book explores new facets of public image, and is a must-have for every PR practitioner's library."

—Margot Winick, college communicator and marketer, and PR professor

"With the exponential growth of the internet, one of the most important issues facing attorneys today is protecting their online reputation. It is a call I receive almost weekly: 'How do I deal with false, negative online reviews?' John David is always my first call, and this book is a must-read for anyone who relies on the internet for business."

—Brian Tannebaum, criminal/ethics defense lawyer and author of *The Practice*

How To Protect (or Destroy) Your Reputation Online

How To Protect (or Destroy) Your Reputation Online

THE ESSENTIAL GUIDE TO
AVOID DIGITAL DAMAGE,
LOCK DOWN YOUR BRAND,
AND **DEFEND** YOUR BUSINESS

JOHN P. DAVID

CAREER
PRESS
Wayne, N.J.

HOW TO PROTECT (OR DESTROY) YOUR REPUTATION ONLINE
EDITED BY PATRICIA KOT
TYPESET BY KARA KUMPEL
Cover design by Ty Nowicki
Printed in the U.S.A.

To order this title, please call toll-free 1-800-CAREER-1 (NJ and Canada: 201-848-0310) to order using VISA or MasterCard, or for further information on books from Career Press.

The Career Press, Inc.
12 Parish Drive
Wayne, NJ 07470
www.careerpress.com

Library of Congress Cataloging-in-Publication Data
CIP Data Available Upon Request.

To Pamela, Emma, and Jack.

Acknowledgments

Though writing is a solitary task, this book would not have been realized without the help and encouragement of many people, particularly my family. My wife, Pamela, steadfastly supports my career in public relations and encourages my writing, whether it be for my blog or this book. She gave me valuable advice at many key moments during the process, and without her, this project would have been impossible. My children, Emma and Jack, were enthusiastic about the book and rearranged parts of their schedules so that I could carve out extra placid moments to finish the manuscript.

I also owe many thanks to my new friends and colleagues in the publishing world. Writer and editor Thomas Hauck provided excellent feedback on my first draft as well as my book proposal, and he pulled back the curtain of the publishing industry, helping me turn a fanciful thought into a reality. My agent, Jeff Herman, took a shot on a first-time author and guided me through the process, answering many questions and allaying all of my concerns. He pitched hard and advocated for me, and I couldn't have asked for more. Adam Schwartz, Lauren Manoy, and the executives at Career Press believed in my book and helped mold its contents into a more complete and useful work, and cover designer Jeff Piasky created the universally loved shield emblem.

As I worked on this, several people were very giving of their time and granted informative interviews. Darnell Holloway at Yelp, Scott Dobroski at Glassdoor, and the executives at TripAdvisor each gave me great insight into best practices at their respective sites and patiently answered my many questions. Adam Sperling of the Hotel Commonwealth and Jay Sofer of LockBusters provided incredible background on working with the review sites and allowed me to feature them as case studies. Cybersecurity expert Brook Zimmatore of Massive offered a detailed education on numerous areas of online reputation management, and famed entrepreneur Mark Cuban graciously agreed to allow republication of my prior interview with him about online privacy.

My father, Tom David, and my brother, Chris David, helped me navigate the contracts, and my friend and unofficial consigliere Jason Margulies offered advice and perspective from the outset of the project. My blogging buddies, Bruce Turkel and David Altshuler, have regularly offered meaningful advice and reassurance for my blog—without which this book would not have happened. I also owe gratitude to the editors at the *Huffington Post* and *PR Daily* who enjoy my quirky take on public relations and marketing, enabling my posts to find a larger audience on their websites.

And lastly, I'm blessed that many people throughout my life, from teachers and professors to friends and colleagues, have encouraged me and told me that I'm a good writer. I often put on a haughty act about my writing, but I don't always believe it. To all of you, I'm humbled and thankful.

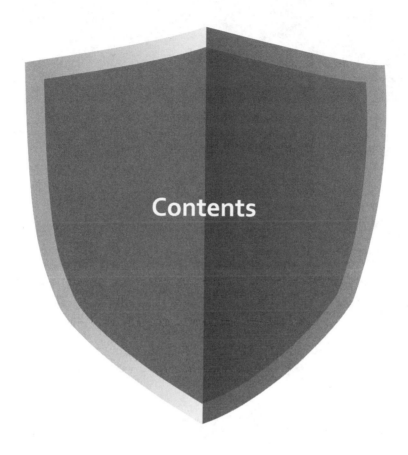

Contents

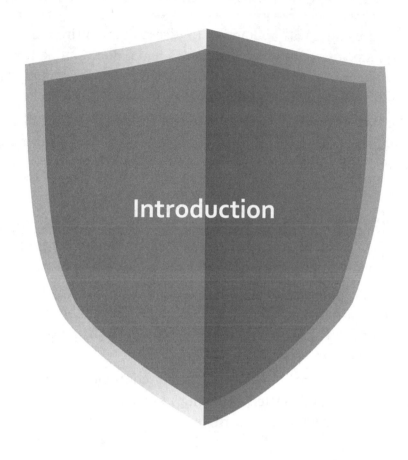

Introduction

My interest in the field of online reputation management was triggered by an event in 2013. While I was on vacation, my brother Chris, an attorney, called and asked if I would be interested in assisting one of his firm's corporate clients, which was facing a public relations crisis. After Chris gave me a brief rundown, I agreed to discuss the issue with one of his law partners.

The next day, as my family and I began our ascent into the North Carolina mountains, I spoke with my brother's colleague and learned that the client was under attack by what can best be described as a rogue blogger. Through a series of sensationalized posts, the blogger was attempting to discredit an entire industry. A few of his posts about other companies had gained online traction, and the client feared irreparable damage to its overall reputation and potentially its entire business if the blogger was left unchecked.

We had to move quickly to mount a defense. While still in the mountains, I was retained and began assisting the attorneys and the client on how to minimize and ultimately prevent damage to the company's reputation.

As I called on my experience from a 20-year career as a public relations consultant to combat this digital assault, I realized that no one is immune to online attacks. Anyone can say practically any-thing online, and sometimes it seems as though there's very little that can be done about it. The situation with the rogue blogger sparked a number of ideas, and for the remainder of my week in the mountains I sketched out a business model to help people facing online reputation issues.

My interest in this emerging problem continued to grow after I returned home and started bouncing my ideas off friends and col-leagues. As I researched, I heard many online horror stories. In fact, nearly every professional person I talked to about my new business idea had dealt with or knew of someone who had an online problem.

This new digital battleground fascinated me because I have strong opinions about what is fair and what is unfair in life—and the internet can be incredibly unfair. It enables people to say almost anything they want, and the door to the online world is wide open for crazy people, mean people, and folks with an axe to grind. In many instances people do stupid things, but sometimes bad things are done to them, and in other cases they're just victims of circum-stance. In too many instances the online punishment goes far past the crime.

Striving to get negative content removed from search results on behalf of my clients has been, without question, one of the most interesting things I have done in my public relations career. And believe me, I have seen some crazy stuff as a public relations guy: environmentalists wanting to free a client's killer whale, highly publicized crises that nearly toppled companies, and even a $100 million Ponzi scheme.

As I developed my own reputation as something of an online fixer, I learned that while a huge number of people and companies have issues with our digital world, too many of them remain unsure about how to prevent or manage these issues. The internet plays a major role in how we are perceived, and many of the public relations challenges facing people and businesses today have to do with online issues.

What has followed is a fascinating ride that is sometimes scary, oftentimes entertaining, and always educational. I would love to say that *How to Protect (Or Destroy) Your Reputation Online* represents a comprehensive manual on dealing with online issues, but I have learned during the course of writing the book that being comprehensive in this field is impossible and impractical. The internet is changing and shifting at such a rapid rate that new opportunities to attack people online will continue to emerge, so we mainly have to understand today's issues while waiting on and trying to anticipate the next wrinkle.

One of the greatest compliments I received for my blogging was from a subscriber who said he enjoyed my practical and actionable take on marketing and public relations. I was flattered because when I write, I try to give it to you straight—and this philosophy has served me well in life and business.

So here's the straight scoop: This book is about vulnerabilities and how we address them. For individuals, both young and old, the book acknowledges that we all make mistakes, and we will continue to make them. Yet it will teach you to understand online vulnerabilities, how to build a reputational firewall, and how to protect yourself. The book discusses the different types of online nightmares, how to handle them, and hopefully how to prevent them. Some of it is common sense (the best defense to your reputation is keeping your nose clean), and other aspects are counterintuitive (you don't get to just stay off the grid). It will teach you how the proliferation of digital cameras in mobile phones, surveillance devices, drones, and even standard-issue police equipment makes us vulnerable.

It will also explain what options you have when facing an online problem. Unfortunately, in recent years, the term "reputation management" was hijacked by search engine optimization specialists who have redefined it to mean the act of pushing down, or suppressing, negative content by flooding the internet with positive and sometimes meaningless information. This book explains that other options exist, from engaging websites directly to the covert ops of reputation management where high-tech experts make content literally disappear from search results.

For businesses, online vulnerabilities are often multiplied. Customers and employees are rating businesses (and even CEOs) on review sites—and sometimes the companies don't even know it. Online complaint sites cause major damage with the help of anonymous reviewers and the veil of freedom of speech. Unseen problems may lurk in the misunderstood deep web and more nefarious activity can be found on the dark web. *How to Protect (Or Destroy) Your Reputation Online* explains these threats and also offers recommendations on how to handle them—often with advice that comes directly from the review sites and those who have worked with them successfully. Business owners and executives will also find guidance on social media policies, traditional media policies, and how to monitor and manage negative online content.

Lastly, this book explains the many ways that companies and individuals can build their online reputation using marketing tactics with other benefits. It turns out that protecting your online reputation can be good for business and for your career.

I hope you find my advice practical and actionable. I wish you only a sterling online reputation. And I hope you keep your nose clean.

—John P. David

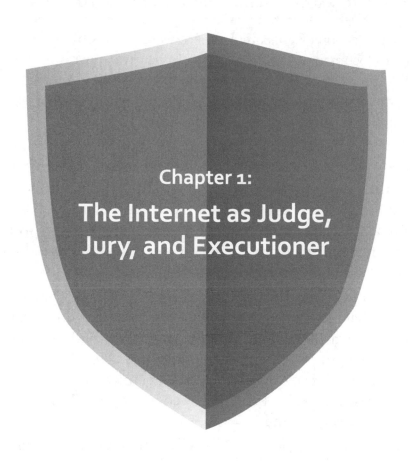

Chapter 1:

The Internet as Judge, Jury, and Executioner

Sitting in a restaurant with a friend recently, I asked a simple question: How many cameras are in this place? He looked up and immediately pointed out several domes scattered around the ceiling of the restaurant. While he had successfully identified the surveillance cameras and confidently guessed that there were about 10 of them, he had fallen right into my trap.

I asked, what about the cell phone cameras of the customers and employees? He frowned as we upped the count to likely north of 50.

At that moment, if a customer were to try to sneak off with a pastry, steal someone's wallet, or go on an epic rant about the price of an extra scoop of guacamole, there were dozens of people at the ready to document it. And this is true in nearly every restaurant and retail store in the United States. Whether we like it or not, at any given moment we are either being actively watched or could be the subject of someone's cell phone video.

We know that it is easy to publish information online, but today photographic and video footage of nearly everything proliferates. This visual scrutiny will only grow. By 2017 there will be more than 200 million smartphones in the United States.[1] (The U.S. population is around 320 million, by the way.) And the average American can be caught on a surveillance camera more than 75 times a day.[2]

Many people have installed video cameras outside their homes, enabling them to see who's knocking on their front door, monitor their yard or driveway, and presumably deter would-be thieves. I even know a guy who has cameras inside his home. They came in handy when his former girlfriend assaulted him. It was a he-said, she-said case until video footage showed her repeatedly hitting him, not the other way around.

Law enforcement agencies have widely adopted dashboard cameras on police cars, and wearable body cameras are next. A friend of mine who happens to be a federal law enforcement agent told me that many police officers initially objected to dashboard cameras, but over time, they have provided valuable evidence that has protected officers' lives and careers. Today, he said, many officers won't go on the street in a patrol car that doesn't have a fully functioning dash cam. Wearable cameras, he believes, will likely be treated similarly and also begin to proliferate.

And what about drones? Unmanned aerial vehicles continue to grow in popularity among hobbyists and security professionals alike. In 2016, the FAA announced that drone registrations in the United States eclipsed those of regular planes.[3] Very soon, there could be more camera-carrying drones in the skies than piloted planes. For well under $100, you can purchase a toy drone equipped with a camera that's capable of spying on your neighbors. My son had one that he used to take footage of our home from about 60 feet up before a sudden breeze and a bad sense of direction sent it sailing off into the wild blue yonder, never to be seen again. We didn't spy on the neighbors, but we could have.

Restaurants, retail stores, banks, government buildings, and even your neighbors are equipped with cameras, so if you're walking your dog, depositing your paycheck, or just grabbing a cup of coffee, there may be video evidence of it somewhere.

As many of us have seen, camera phones capture fascinating still and moving pictures every day. In its advertising, Apple brags about the quality of its iPhone cameras, and Go Pro cameras document even the most harrowing situations in high definition brilliance.

Cameras capture the good and the bad, the cop and the robber, the perpetrator and the victim. Because of this proliferation, people get photographed and filmed doing bad things: underage kids drinking beer, of-age celebs taking bong hits, and stupid people doing what they do best. Accused murderer Aaron Hernandez was filmed by *his own home security cameras* holding a gun both before and after the killing of Odin Lloyd. The images became evidence against him.

Now don't get me wrong; I'm not anti-technology or a privacy zealot. Widespread usage of these cameras also does tremendous good. Following the Boston Marathon bombing, federal officials were able to compile surveillance footage that showed Dzhokhar Tsarnaev dropping his homemade pressure cooker bomb among the crowd. Between the camera phone and surveillance footage, the entire bombing was catalogued with convincing accuracy. In this case, the proliferation of public cameras helped capture and convict a murderous terrorist.

A number of cultural shifts have contributed to making it so much easier for us to be seen doing something illegal, stupid, silly, or just embarrassing. First, digital cameras with high resolution can be very small. With a device that can fit in the palm of your hand—or even be embedded in your eyeglasses—you can secretly photograph or videotape someone doing something criminal or just having a bad day, like the person who loses it at the post office, cable provider, office, or restaurant (regarding the aforementioned guacamole).

Second, you can share your video or photo with the world. "Citizen journalists" can speedily upload an interesting photo or video to the web or send it to a bona fide media outlet. Many of us are guilty of paparazzi-like tendencies when we see a famous person. Friends of mine have posted images on Facebook of celebrities including Ashton Kutcher and Paul McCartney. I have to admit that if I saw a Beatle on the street, I would try to get a photo too. Lastly, we are in the middle of the era of viral marketing. Many would consider it a badge of honor for one of their photos, gifs, memes, or videos to get shared with thousands of people. So we are seeking out and even manufacturing opportunities to grab our 15 minutes of fame, even if it's at the expense of another human being.

The Internet: Where Bad News Can Stay Forever

Did you know that David Geffen lied on his first job application? The 2012 documentary *Inventing David Geffen* details the life of the billionaire entertainment mogul who has many legendary accomplishments, including putting the Eagles and Jackson Browne on vinyl, *Cats* and *Dreamgirls* on Broadway, and *Risky Business* and *Interview With the Vampire* on movie screens. One of the many anecdotes Geffen shares in the documentary is about his first job at the William Morris Agency in New York. He lied on his application for a mailroom position at the talent agency, stating that he had graduated from UCLA. The agency hired him and put him to work, but they did this before they had checked his credentials with UCLA. With Geffen already on the payroll, the agency sent an inquiry to UCLA via old-fashioned postal mail.

After learning that a fellow employee had been fired for lying on his application, Geffen began inspecting every piece of mail coming into William Morris. (After all, he was working in the mailroom!) When the incriminating letter from UCLA arrived, he steamed it opened and altered its contents. The rest is blockbuster history.

Today's job applicants can't use the same solution as Geffen. Employers may instantly check credentials by using Google searches, and they're looking for a lot more than proof of matriculation. I have fielded dozens of calls from individuals, both young and old, who have had problems getting jobs due to online issues.

I once heard from a dentist who had been happily leading his life. In his past there was a very small criminal offense that had long been forgotten. He chose to apply for a job with a major corporate player in the dental world, and while checking his own online profile, he found reference to the misdeed from 20 years earlier: He and a few of his fraternity brothers had been charged with smoking marijuana during a protest on the Washington Mall. The dentist feared that if his prospective employer learned of the listing, he might have lost out on the job.

An attorney was fired from a law firm job and disbarred for overbilling clients. He tried to reinvent himself as a consultant but couldn't hold a job because web listings of his problems were easily found online. As soon as he started to climb the ranks at a new company, a copy of the story of his disbarment would be slid under the door of his employer, and he'd find himself out of work. He dealt with this for more than 10 years.

A young lady reached out to me because there were some unflattering (yet thankfully not pornographic) photos of her online. Debbie was still in college and appeared to be a bit of a party girl. When you searched her name, a number of photos showed up that looked as though they were taken at night clubs. In one photo, she had her tongue out and was giving the "double bird" to the camera. In cities with active club scenes, roaming photographers move about clubs taking photos of the guests, which they later post online. If the club-goer wants to memorialize their night out, they can purchase a picture. In most cases, the photos are posted without names or other identification. So, if you were out last Friday night at Club XYZ, you can visit the photography website and see if you like the photos. If you don't like them, your eyes are shut, or you just don't want to pay for a picture of yourself, you don't buy them.

For the young lady, it turned out that one of the photographers knew her and had tagged her name to one of the photos. That's all it took. Google did the rest. Photo identification technology may have contributed to it, and so may have Google's love of images in search results.

Regardless, on page one of her search results, an image appeared of the young lady flipping both middle fingers. Fast-forward a year or two, and she was preparing to apply for summer internships. It was not a good situation. I urged her to contact the photography company and to be relentless about it. Eventually the photo came down.

You Will Be Googled

If you're applying for a job, it's best to assume that prospective employers will be checking you out online. You will be Googled. I've seen statistics stating that up to 90 percent of employers research applicants online, and they don't stop with Google. A CareerBuilder study in 2014 found that more than 40 percent of employers review applicants' social media accounts, and more than half found information that caused them not to hire an applicant.[4]

Here's a sample of what recruiters most commonly find on social media that knocks a prospective employee out of contention:

- provocative or inappropriate photographs or information
- information about them drinking or using drugs
- posts that bad-mouth previous employers or coworkers

- posts displaying poor communication skills
- discriminatory comments related to race, gender, religion, etc.
- lies about qualifications
- unprofessional screen names

I spoke with a friend who runs a successful executive search firm. He told me that negative online information can remove a candidate from contention for jobs at the highest levels. He said that when you see that type of information online, "sometimes you just have to punt" and move on to the next applicant.

Anyone in the workforce who wants to have a long and successful career needs to look good online. We can't all be David Geffen and be worth nearly $7 billion, but we can start at the bottom and work our way up—as long as we can get that first opportunity.

One day, Susan, a client of my public relations firm, called in a panic. One of Susan's college-aged children was peripherally involved with a crisis at her university. A group of students had been accused of some overly raucous behavior at a school-related event, and it eventually received national media attention. The allegations, later proved largely false, had drawn the ire of the university as well a number of opinion leaders and commentators. It had potential to get completely out of control.

Susan and some of the other parents were wondering if it would be beneficial to engage a public relations expert. They had many questions. Should they reach out to the media? How might their kids be perceived?

Before we dug into the details of the incident, I told Susan that the very first thing that needed to be done was to ensure that the students did not say anything about the incident that might end up online. I cautioned her: Don't post anything about it on Facebook, don't tweet about it, and absolutely do not speak to anyone from the media. I told Susan that the most important thing was to guarantee that her child's name was in no way associated online with this situation. She needed to keep her kid's name shielded from this crisis so that the student would not be associated with it in any way—pro, con, or indifferent. This crisis, I counseled, would eventually pass, but an online connection to it could last forever.

Because the internet is now king, we're in a whole new world of crisis management.

More and more situations arise where people are literally in the wrong place at the wrong time and end up crucified online. They find themselves with a massive problem that they are in no position to solve.

Here's another example. I spoke with a young man who, while in college, worked as an assistant manager for one of the university's shops. While Charles worked there, the full-time head of the shop passed away unexpectedly. A subsequent audit found that money was missing, and the police were called to investigate the embezzlement.

As part of the investigation, they questioned Charles. It's important to note that he was *questioned*, not *arrested*. He complied with the police and even turned over his laptop for their review. After they checked him out, the cops determined he had no connection to the missing money, and he was completely cleared.

Meanwhile, the university newspaper wrote a story about the embezzlement and mentioned that Charles had been questioned by police. Fast-forward a couple of years. Charles had graduated and was trying to get a job, but he couldn't even get an interview.

Here's the problem: When you searched for his name, the online version of the story appeared on the first page of the search engine results. Charles was in finance, and whenever he applied for a job, he was researched online and prospective employers saw his name associated with an embezzlement case. Charles was screwed.

If you were a human resources manager, would you give him a fair shake? All things being equal among candidates, which applicant would be more likely to get an interview: an applicant with a spotless reputation or one who had been questioned about embezzlement? What if you had to quickly screen dozens of candidates? When left unchecked, the internet can be the judge, jury, and executioner of your reputation.

The important thing to understand is that yesterday's public relations strategies aren't sufficient to combat the damage done by the internet. Charles had a crisis of perception on his hands, and it was nothing like any of the classic case studies covered in a public relations course syllabus. Perhaps the most significant characteristic of online negativity is that it can be viewed by anyone *forever*. It doesn't fade away.

When we encounter a crisis, we need to quickly determine what the online legacy will be and then develop a strategy to prevent negative coverage from the onset. Understanding that something stated online (whether true or not) can be damning for years to come is absolutely critical.

Negative online articles and stories can be mitigated and, in some instances, completely removed, but this process is expensive when done after the fact and not always possible. The big takeaway is that if you are associated with something negative, either directly, indirectly, or just by accident, the online reporting of it can affect you for years to come. The problem must be managed as quickly and aggressively as possible.

The Tweet Heard 'Round the World

Late during the evening of December 20, 2013, I took a peek at my Twitter feed and noticed that a marketing guy whom I follow named Peter Shankman was pleading for some internet sanity regarding a woman named Justine Sacco. The woman in question was at that moment comfortably seated on an 11-hour flight from London to Cape Town, South Africa. Even as her plane was in the air, all of Twitterdom was exploding. Peter said in his tweet, "Yes,

[Sacco's] tweet was awful. But she's landing to death threats. Come on, Twitter, let's be better than that."

Intrigued, I typed her name into the search bar and began decoding what was happening. Sacco had indeed written an awful tweet. The exact words were "Going to Africa. Hope I don't get AIDS. Just kidding. I'm white." She had apparently written it just before leaving on her flight from London to South Africa. As the plane cruised at 30,000 feet, Sacco had no idea of the firestorm her tweet had created. Many on Twitter were rightly offended and started to attack her online while she was still mid-flight. Her employer disavowed her before her plane touched down. It's quite possible that Sacco, who was indeed fired from her job as corporate public relations pro, was sacked in mid-air, and hundreds of thousands of people knew about it before she did. Talk about a collision of old world technology and new world communications.

One thing that struck me was the reaction of the Twitter universe. If you had watched the real-time feed of comments about Sacco, you would have witnessed thousands of tweets per hour and the formation of an online mob. Granted, some of the online salvos were meant in jest (and there were some funny ones), but many people were really angry and had no problem unloading their venom on the defenseless Sacco.

Had she written the same tweet but had not been on a transcontinental flight sans Wi-Fi, the outcome could have been different. She could have quickly deleted the offending tweet before it went viral and perhaps salvaged her job. To her credit, Sacco later apologized.

Companies can do dumb things too. On April 14, 2014, a public relations person at US Airways responded to a routine customer complaint with a tweet. The tweet said, "We welcome feedback, Elle. If your travel is complete, you can detail here for review and follow up." The tweet included a link. Through some ghastly error or malicious scheme, the link led to an obscene photograph of a naked woman pleasuring herself with a model jet airplane. It took almost a full hour before the company removed the tweet, and by that time it had blazed a trail through the internet.

The company sent out a follow-up tweet after the original image garnered more than 500 retweets: "We apologize for an inappropriate image recently shared as a link in one of our responses. We've removed the tweet and are investigating."

By that time, it had been called "the worst tweet in the history of Twitter." How did it happen? No one knows for sure, but one scenario is that a hacker exploited a security vulnerability to grab US Airways' Twitter password and posted the pic as an act of maliciousness.

Do bad tweets last forever? Just Google "US Airways tweet" and see for yourself.

The Internet Didn't Invent Being Mean; It Just Perfected It

While online shaming, revenge porn, and hate blogs may be new concepts, being mean-spirited and hateful are not. I'm sure cavemen got mad at their neighbors. They just didn't have the Twitter accounts (or the alphabet) necessary to broadcast their hate. And I'm certain that the teenagers I knew when I was in high school could be just as nasty as they can be today. My generation just lacked Wi-Fi and viral videos. The internet didn't invent mean, but it sure is perfecting it.

One of the benefits of being born and raised during the analog age is that I was able to witness the digital revolution firsthand. Like anyone born in or before the 1960s, I remember the time before the internet, mobile phones, texting, and social media. In the early 1990s, when I started my business career, the fax machine was king, FedEx was booming because you could send an original document anywhere in the country overnight, and there were squadrons of bike messengers working the streets. The digital age would soon change everything.

I remember when I first learned about the internet in the 1990s. My friend Todd Kocourek, a brilliant international attorney and altogether forward thinker, sat me down at his computer. After logging on through a dial-up phone modem, he started showing me web pages. We marveled at how, at that time, government agencies were posting thousands and thousands of pages of public information online. Todd knew it would change the world and tried to convey this to a public relations guy who was very young and not yet tech savvy.

In the early days, just to access web pages you had to have a certain amount of wherewithal: a computer with the right amount of firepower, a modem to access the web with your phone line, and the ability to acquire and install one of the early internet web browsers. Broadband and routers were years away, and nothing was "plug and play." If you were successful at aligning all the steps to get online, it still didn't always work right.

And this was just to access the internet to see and read content. Creating online content was no easy trick. The first website project I worked on in the mid-1990s was a major undertaking. Very few regular folks understood the technology or the nomenclature. Having your own domain was a pipe dream, as most of us didn't know how all the pieces went together. Google, Yahoo, Twitter, and Facebook were years away from existence. The term "blog" hadn't yet been created. Technical barriers prevented most of us from posting anything at all online, much less something like an online attack. In those early days, there was no user-friendly vehicle for posting your own content online.

The internet was literally uncharted territory. I actually remember talking to the first internet service provider whom I ever met and saying, "The guy who figures out how to create the Yellow Pages of the internet would make a lot of money." Looking back, I realize it was a huge understatement.

Almost from its infancy, the internet was identified as a forum for anonymous disparagement. While we think of online attacks as being a relatively new phenomenon, some enterprising folks identified the web as an attack platform early on. In the same year that Google was officially founded, 1998, so was the online complaint site RipoffReport.com. The site—which still operates today—allowed consumers to post complaints about providers of goods or services. The target of the complaint was allowed to post a rebuttal. It was an open forum for nastiness.

Today, we take for granted that we can publish information to the web in a matter of seconds, and we know that our lives are enriched by the internet. Because of Facebook, I've reconnected with dozens of people with whom I had lost contact over the years. LinkedIn has created business opportunities for me that have led to direct revenue for my company. I have online reputation clients in China and Australia. And my own blogging activities have led to career opportunities and have played a major role in my efforts to write this very book.

Communications have been democratized so anyone can say whatever they want, whenever they want. The downside is that anyone can say whatever they want, whenever they want. The internet's blessings are bittersweet.

The growth of social media, blogging platforms, and complaint sites have made it all too easy to post negative information online. Using social media sites like Facebook and Twitter, the general public regularly passes judgment on people and events. We have even begun to expect it. If a political candidate makes a misstep, for example, one of the first places we look for public reaction is the social media universe. If anyone, even a previously anonymous person, makes a major public mistake, you can almost expect there to be an internet reaction. And of course, media celebrities can purposefully "break the internet"—or at least get millions of views—by posting sensational material.

Blogging platforms like Blogger, Tumblr, and WordPress have made it very easy to get online and start communicating. While the vast majority of bloggers are attempting to reach a core audience with authentic and genuine communications, others are simply online to promote misinformation and hate.

Complaint sites like RipoffReport.com and others have made it simple for anyone with an e-mail account to post an online complaint about a company or individual. If you have a legitimate beef with a company with whom you have transacted business, these sites are conceptually valuable. The problem is that these sites let anyone post to them with little regard for the truth. Such sites make money based on the volume of content and resultant ad revenue, so they take little to no effort to verify the veracity of complaints.

Some people are using our newly democratized communication channels to practice online extremism. Consider how simple it is to create an anonymous and practically untraceable hate blog. Anyone can do it in three easy steps:

1. Visit a website like Google, Yahoo, or AOL and secure a new, nondescript e-mail address.

2. Use that e-mail address to create blog on a site like Blogger or Tumblr.

3. Start writing malicious content about your chosen victim.

Within no time, the posts can start appearing high on search results, particularly if the victim doesn't have a strong online reputation. If the perpetrator is clever enough and mean enough, the site can cause an immense amount of reputational damage and even disrupt the professional or personal life of the victim. A similar strategy could be employed to attack a business using an online complaint site, and again, the perpetrator can be anonymous and hidden.

Technology hasn't made us meaner, but it is now much easier to be mean.

The Three Types of Online Nightmares

One of the first things I learned about online reputation issues is that no two are exactly alike. Of course, there are many common threads, but each instance always seems to be unique in some way. People get punished online for behavior that one person might find reprehensible while another person might just shrug it off.

While each incident has unique qualities, I've found that most online reputation issues fall into one of three general categories:

1. People doing dumb things
2. People being associated with negative things
3. People being victimized

Some of the lines of demarcation are fuzzy, and online issues often touch multiple categories. The one commonality is that people and organizations suffer in some way due to the issue—because anyone can now learn about their problem using one of the millions of devices connected to the internet.

People Doing Dumb Things

The vast majority of online issues arise from a situation where someone does something morally, ethically, or legally wrong. They get arrested for soliciting a prostitute, which is then reported in the local newspaper. They are cited for driving under the influence, and the arrest is publicized. Executives take part in a business venture with some shady characters, and journalists and bloggers chime in or publish incriminating information. Lawyers and stockbrokers lose their licenses and learn that news of this will be on a regulatory agency's website forever. People pose for photographs, flipping off the camera (or worse), and may not even remember it until the image is dominating their search results.

Consider the story of U.S. Representative Anthony Weiner. On May 27, 2011, using his public Twitter account, Weiner sent a link to a 21-year-old female college student from Seattle, Washington, who was following Weiner's posts. The link led to a photo that Weiner had posted to a social networking platform called yfrog. The photo showed a man wearing boxer shorts in a sexually excited condition. Though the link was quickly removed from Weiner's Twitter account, screen shots of the congressman's original message and the photo were captured by a user identified as Dan Wolfe, who sent them to conservative blogger Andrew Breitbart. The following day, Breitbart published them on his BigGovernment website.

From that moment, Weiner's career went straight downhill. Other online photos surfaced, and on June 20, he resigned his seat in Congress. Later, he said that if the year had been 1952 and there were no internet, the whole thing never would have happened.

A gentleman once reached out to me who had made a poor choice. An unmarried technology consultant, Julian lived in the United States under a work visa, and one evening he sought the company of a lady for hire. Unfortunately for him, he solicited an undercover police officer who was part of a local crackdown on prostitution. To publicize their crackdown, the police issued a news release to local media outlets, publishing the names of all those who had been arrested as part of their sting.

Within a few weeks of his arrest, when you typed Julian's name in the search bar, several stories about the event appeared on the first few pages of search results. Our wayward soul, who would have been doing nothing wrong had he been in one of eight counties in Nevada, was forced to manage a reputational crisis while trying to explain his arrest and indiscretion to his friends and family. To make matters worse, his consulting contracts were typically several months in length, so he needed to regularly secure new engagements. Each time he needed to find a new job, prospective employers Googled his name. Without assistance, his entire life—his personal relationships, his ability to earn a living, and his reputation—were at risk of ruin.

Did the reputational punishment fit the crime? I thought not, and I had no problem helping Julian repair his reputation. I'll reveal later how we handled it using an online reputation tactic called suppression.

The internet had meted out a tremendous penalty to Julian, and the penalty had a long life. In the old days, such negative information would have been published in the newspaper, and at the end of the day everyone threw away their papers. The following day you'd get a fresh newspaper delivered to your doorstep, and it would be likely that the story that mentioned you would be gone. As each day went by, your story would fade further into the unreachable past. If someone wanted to research your past misbehavior, they'd have to go to the library and find the microfilm of the old issue of the newspaper. Today, the digital record of the report can stay online for decades and be instantly accessible with the click of a mouse.

A lady reached out to me with a similar problem. Isabel was found early one morning sleeping in her car (albeit parked partially on the sidewalk), and she failed a field sobriety test. She was guilty, but no one was injured, thankfully. A local newspaper, with public information provided by the police department, reported on her arrest. This wayward soul was tremendously embarrassed and repentant, but the search results negatively impacted her business long after she had paid her dues to the criminal justice system. She dealt with the legal side of the event but had an online reputation issue to contend with as well.

Each day, thousands of people have similar problems where they did something wrong, the event became part of the public record, and the internet and search engines negatively impacted their lives. In some cases, internet searches find old information that some folks think is long forgotten.

Karen had a bad debt with a credit card company, and the judgment was posted online. She was a social media professional, so a huge part of her life was lived online. The judgment was a major embarrassment and appeared in the third position on Google results when you searched her name.

Edie, a respected executive, was involved with a difficult lawsuit with a former business partner. She eventually moved from the East Coast to the Pacific Northwest and started a new company. The lawsuit filing, posted on a state government website, appeared as the first item on Google when you searched her name, even though it had been settled years earlier.

Andrew reached out to me because he was concerned about some pictures on the internet. The images appeared on the search results when you Googled his nickname. Andrew, it turned out, had a very large asset of the personal nature, and there were many photos of him—and it—online on a variety of websites. A girl he was dating, and wanted to continue dating, had found the pictures. He was embarrassed.

I said that I was sorry he was dealing with this, but hey, there are worse things to be known for in life, right? I Googled his real name, and none of the photos appeared. Apparently, the racy shots had been tagged using only his nickname.

I leveled with him. There were more than 20 listings online that showed these images. If we were to develop a plan to get these links removed, it would probably cost tens of thousands of dollars, if not more. Andrew was a young blue-collar worker, and this was clearly not an option.

My advice was:

1. Ditch the nickname.
2. Cease and desist taking or allowing people to take pictures of his junk.

Sounds like a no-brainer, right? Andrew didn't like my advice about his nickname. "I can't get rid of my nickname," he implored. I asked why not. Apparently, he had a lot invested in the nickname and a lot of folks knew him because of it. Turns out that it was also his Facebook handle.

I gave it to him straight. "I understand you like your nickname," I said, "but anyone who searches for you online in the future may end up getting a lot more of you than you want. If Sean John Combs can become Puff Daddy and then P. Diddy and still be worth half a billion dollars, then you can drop your nickname."

Andrew considered my advice, and he soon dropped the nickname.

People Being Associated with a Negative Event

Some online problems are thrust upon us, such as the situation with the young man who worked at the campus store. In other cases, someone close to us personally or professionally makes a mistake that impacts us. And in some instances, the internet connects virtual dots and the results create a problem.

A gentleman who called me was the CEO of a well-respected family business. Paul's company operated throughout the United States and, by all methods of measure, had a pristine reputation. Then his namesake son was arrested for marijuana possession on a company job site. According to one news report, officers saw smoke billowing from a trailer. Now, had this occurred in Colorado, for example, it would be no big deal, but Paul Jr. had chosen to light up in a state where it was a no-no.

News of the arrest of Paul's son was publicized on several news sites, and you can imagine that the father, who shared the same name, was none too pleased. When you typed their shared name into Google, news of the drug bust appeared prominently on the first page of search results. It was both embarrassing and damaging.

Here's another one. A young man who was under the legal drinking age went out with friends and was served a beer. One of his friends took a group photo and the underage kid was tagged on Facebook. Without even knowing it, a picture of him drinking had been posted online for his friends, relatives, and college admissions officers to see. Making matters worse, the underage drinker was dependent on his friend to take it down.

Sometimes, online troubles can seem to be randomly generated. Richard was a Vietnam veteran and a recipient of the Silver Star. One day he did a Google search and found his name and that of his military unit were prominently displayed on a porn site. Perplexed and offended, he called me.

Pornography is a $100 billion business globally, and in the United States it is bigger than the NFL, the NBA, and MLB combined. Some of the most sophisticated internet marketers in the world work for porn sites, and they often prey upon successful and popular search terms. If a porn marketer thinks they can drive traffic to one of its sites by hijacking the pristine reputation of a guy like Richard, they will do it in a heartbeat. Because I love my country and appreciate what our veterans have done for those of us who get to patriotically drive desks in the land of the free, I gave him some advice at no charge.

Google strives to give us the best possible search results, I explained. The brainiacs in Mountain View, California, want us to find what we are looking for when we search, and if we don't want porn, we shouldn't see it in our search results. To that end, Google has a section on its support site dedicated to this very thing. If your name or your business name is on a porn site, and a few other conditions are met, then Google will remove that page from its search engine. I directed our war hero to this page. He filled out the form, and a few days later the offending link was gone.

On another occasion, a very nice lady called me because she was dealing with something truly awful. Her grown son had been killed a few years earlier, but that day when she typed his name into Google, a listing appeared that included his Social Security number and birthdate. So aside from having to deal with the loss of her son, she was very troubled that someone could very easily steal his identity. I directed her to the appropriate Google support page dedicated to preventing government-issued identification numbers from being shared online. She submitted the offending link and it was removed from search results.

Sometimes the internet's super powers cause hurt. A gentleman reached out to me with a request that I found odd at the time. When Timothy did a Google search of his mobile phone number, his number appeared on a site whose mission was to combat telemarketing. Timothy wanted it removed because it appeared as though he was a pushy telemarketer. It turned out that many people do reverse phone number searches. This one had labeled him as a "scammer" even though he had never telemarketed anyone.

Another guy, who was indeed a bit shifty, reached out to me because the internet had connected two of his companies, and he preferred that the world didn't know of any affiliation. As best as I could tell, Jack would buy goods with one company and then broker the sale of the same goods for his customers using another company. One of his customers did some online snooping and identified his scheme as a means to charge additional markup for the goods.

People Being Victimized

In my humble opinion, the worst situations occur when a perpetrator inflicts online damage upon an innocent victim. The ease of putting information online fuels the fire, as do companies that have figured out how to make money from online suffering.

Few things can do more damage to the online reputation of a person or organization than a hate blog. Often created anonymously and sometimes by very web-savvy individuals, a negative blog can poison the search engine results of even the most sophisticated individuals and businesses.

The word "blog" is a shortened form of the term "web log," and it was first coined in the late 1990s. Blogs were originally thought of as simple online diaries. They were first written by individuals who memorialized their lives and pontificated on a number of subjects. Blogs were esoteric in the early days, but then some clever entrepreneurs created easy-to-use blogging platforms like Blogger, Tumblr, and WordPress, making it very simple for anyone to blog. Blogger, the platform, was later purchased by Google, helping bring blogging to the masses.

Some blog sites have morphed into bona fide news sites, such as the *Huffington Post* or Nate Silver's *FiveThirtyEight*. Others remain simple homespun entertainment and hobbyist websites. The blog has truly helped democratize communication around the world. Yet as many have quickly figured out, freedom of expression may be embraced by people who may not be happy with certain businesses or other people.

Sometimes the hate blog is completely out in the open. We have seen scorned lovers sign their names to blogs as they proudly bash their ex-wives, husbands, boyfriends, or girlfriends. The blogger secures some personal solace in expressing their feelings (typically hostile) for all to read on the web. Others are anonymous, which makes them somewhat less credible. Either way, hate blogs have a tendency to cause major stress for the victims.

In one case, an executive who ran a small publicly traded company was so victimized by a hate blog that he literally erased his involvement with the company from his resume. Like many companies during the last recession, his company had imploded under financial strain and many investors lost money. One particularly upset individual decided to create an anonymous hate blog that compared the executive to a popular cartoon character. When you searched the executive's name and the company, the first listing on Google search was the hate blog. The executive, who also lost a considerable amount of money with the company's demise, suffered so much reputational damage from the blog that he decided it was easier not to have his stint as a CEO as a line on his resume.

In another case, a successful executive found himself in a bad relationship with an extremely bitter yet web-savvy woman. Rick said one thing and she said another—but she said it online, and all of a sudden, he was trying to explain what happened to his friends and family, who were seeing salacious accusations online that were now dominating search results for his name.

Later in the book we'll learn how he used a number of tactics, including the "covert ops" of reputation management, to solve his problem.

Some hate blogs do their damage with the author in plain sight. Raymond is the owner of a construction company in the northeastern United States. He awoke one morning to find that his on-again, off-again girlfriend had started publishing a blog about their relationship. She had much to say. Regular posts about how he had repeatedly hurt her (emotionally) and how he was a lousy human being started appearing a few times per month. (It's important to note that she never accused Raymond of ever physically harming her or even threatening her. At worst, by some standards, he was a jerk.) Raymond, to his credit, tried to repair the relationship and even went to counseling with the woman, who was now definitely his ex. Yet the vitriolic blog posts continued to be published, and the hate blog sat in the second position on Google when you searched Raymond's name. He pleaded with her to take the blog down, but as of this writing she hasn't yet, even after agreeing to do so at the urging of a therapist.

According to Raymond, the blog has caused him to rethink whether he wants to continue living in the same town where he has lived most of his life and where his business is headquartered. "If

I run into her at the grocery store, the next day there's a new blog post," he has lamented to me.

While the details of the blog posts aren't that important to this story, I have to admit that this hate blog perplexes me like no other. What's her motive? Raymond said he once got upset with her because her dogs repeatedly clawed at his leather furniture. He yelled at her, and she found that to be "emotionally abusive." If that's a standard for abuse, most married guys I know are emotionally abused every day, and probably before breakfast.

The ex didn't give up or get bored with her attacks. She commemorated the one-year anniversary of her first blog post by publishing a message featuring an image of a cupcake with one candle in it. Happy birthday to hate.

It's not just blogs that can be damaging. Back in 1998, one of the very first online porn sites was a platform called Seemyex.com. (It's gone now, so don't waste your time looking for it.) Disgruntled people—male or female—could upload private photos of their ex-boyfriend or ex-girlfriend for all the world to see. It was a website of a type that we now call "revenge porn," which I discuss later in the book.

Just Staying off the Grid Is Not an Option

Now that you're sufficiently terrified about what can go wrong, perhaps you think that the best solution might be to avoid the internet and social media altogether. It kind of makes sense, right? Had Justine Sacco not been on Twitter, she wouldn't have gotten herself fired, right? If you don't have Facebook, then you can't be tagged in a photo or post something inappropriate, correct? Not so fast.

It surprises me that many professional people deliberately exert no control over their online reputations. While it's increasingly rare, I meet executives whose companies don't have websites. And many professionals proudly say that they aren't on Facebook or Twitter and don't pay much attention to their LinkedIn profiles. They believe that the less information about them online the better, and this is often paired with the opinion that social media wastes time or is invasive. The strategy—if you can call it that—appears to be that they believe they can control what is said about them online by saying very little. They believe that they can be "off the grid."

But then something goes wrong, and they find themselves knee deep in an online problem without an internet presence to leverage in their defense. This very situation happened to a prominent business consultant. The son of a famous professional athlete, William got himself into trouble. Because he had avoided social media completely and was off the grid, suddenly the only information anyone could see online was this one bad event.

So what did William do? He called an online reputation management company, and they started a suppression campaign. This entailed trying to flood the search engines with positive content about him, which would push down the negative stuff—hopefully.

The first thing the suppression companies did was create social media accounts for him on Facebook, Twitter, LinkedIn, Google+, and so on. Yes, these are the very sites that William had been avoiding while he was out selling his wares, making his millions, and focusing intently on his company.

Unfortunately for William, the negative stories continue to dominate his search results. Without strong social profiles, his situation would become even worse. While William was ignoring social media, these sites had climbed the ranks to become the most authoritative properties on the internet. More people visit Facebook than any other place on the web, and Twitter and LinkedIn are not far behind.

This concept of authority is extremely important when one is dealing with online reputation situations. Your profiles on Facebook and Twitter usually outperform your company site on Google searches. For example, the Twitter page for Warren Buffett pops up at number five on Google, ahead of BerkshireHathaway.com. The Oracle of Omaha opened his Twitter account on May 2, 2013; his first tweet was this: "Warren is in the house."

He quickly amassed over 1.5 million followers. Then, between May 2013 and May 2016, Warren Buffet, posted exactly eight tweets. *Eight.* The Oracle speaks rarely—only eight pronouncements in over two years, with over a million souls waiting breathlessly for the next one.

Whether you're Warren Buffet or Joe the Plumber, social media sites remain a powerful force in influencing search results. Yet in many instances, the online *problem* has a higher authority than your Twitter page—or any other page, for that matter. How Google determines authority in search results is not a topic that I can address; the company says that it constantly changes its highly complex and secret algorithms. What I do know is that, sometimes, a news story or prominent blog post finds a home on page one of your search results, and suppression tactics don't do any good. In this case, you need to engage a specialist who can dig in and look at all possible options—legal, covert ops, or otherwise.

The moral of the story is that being off the grid may seem like a good idea, but it may come back to haunt you if something goes wrong online. Every professional person should take control of their online reputation as a key part of their career advancement strategy.

The Movement to Anonymity

A 2013 study from the Pew internet Research Project titled "Anonymity, Privacy, and Security Online" found that most internet users would like to occasionally be anonymous. The report said that 86 percent of users "have taken steps to remove or mask their digital footprints—ranging from clearing cookies to encrypting their e-mail, from avoiding using their name to using virtual networks that mask their internet protocol (IP) address."[5]

Technology companies have created ways to use the latest techno trappings, but without leaving a digital paper trail. I have often mused that being off the grid and therefore not beholden to technology could become the new status symbol, but in the meantime, some new offerings strive to hide and even erase online activities.

Most of us are aware that we can turn off web browser settings that track our history. Private browsing makes sense when you're using someone else's computer, want to view pages without historical cookies influencing performance, or want to keep your web activity private. A 2012 article by blogger Elie Burzstein suggested that nearly 20 percent of web surfers have used private browsing.[6]

The mobile app Snapchat enables users to share photos and short videos via text message, but the catch is that they disappear after 30 seconds. Originally thought of as a clever way to erase a "sexting" trail, the company is popular for sending selfies, funny pics, and videos, not just illicit stuff. With the ongoing fear that a foolish text might come back to haunt us, perhaps this is a way to avoid future online reputation management problems. With this in mind, it isn't surprising that investors are enthusiastic about its myriad uses: In August 2014, Snapchat received another $20 million in venture capital on top of its other investments, bringing its value up to $10 billion.

The potential to make billions will always inspire competition, and the emergence of Snapchat drew the attention of tech billionaire Mark Cuban. In 2014, the Dallas Mavericks owner and *Shark Tank* star launched Cyber Dust, another text messaging app that—you guessed it—enables you to send texts that disappear and can't be tracked. Cuban says he was inspired by a desire to have online conversations that are more like face-to-face communications. In the offline world, normal one-on-one conversations are not recorded, so after something is said, it's gone. Cuban may have a personal motivation; he has said his text messages have been subpoenaed, misinterpreted, and manipulated by lawyers after the fact.

And then there's GoTenna. This one's not an app but rather a personalized antenna that enables you to send text messages to another person who's equipped with the same device and located within a few miles. Advertising suggests it's a way to stay in touch when traveling in remote areas—like a group of hikers staying connected in an area without cell service. Marketers also say it's a way for friends at a crowded outdoor event, like a concert, to communicate even if the mobile grid is overwhelmed. And according to GoTenna's website, "Messages are end-to-end encrypted and not stored anywhere. They also can be set to self-destruct once the recipient reads it."

Maybe I'm a cynic, but I originally thought there was something sneaky going on. Are we clamoring for ways to communicate more privately, or are these products designed to evade some other form of detection? However, the more I talk with people, the more I discover that many are craving online and offline privacy, and they're worried that an online misstep will hurt them now or in the future. Plus, a $10 billion valuation of Snapchat says the smart money is on this being more trend than fad. Perhaps this digital version of "what happens in Vegas stays in Vegas" will become part of how we all communicate online in the future. We say it—and then it's gone.

Famed Billionaire Chimes in on Online Privacy

It might seem like a contradiction that an executive who's a celebrity with a huge public persona would be blazing trails for online privacy, but billionaire Mark Cuban is doing just that. Cuban, owner of the Dallas Mavericks and a star of CNBC's *Shark Tank,* takes privacy so seriously that he has multiple business interests devoted to helping individuals and companies send and receive messages and post on social media more securely and more privately.

In 2014, after the *Huffington Post* published one of my blog posts in which I mentioned Cuban's mobile app Cyber Dust and the fact that he also invested in Xpire, an app that helps consumers manage and minimize their digital footprints, I reached out to Cuban and asked if he would answer some additional questions about Cyber Dust and online privacy. He graciously agreed, so following are five questions with Cuban about online privacy.

John P. David (JPD): "Cyber Dust launched earlier this year, first on iPhone and later on Android. How's business? Are you hitting your goals? Is your customer base what you expected?"

Mark Cuban (MC): "We're growing far faster than I expected, but I have no idea what our demographics are. We don't ask our users about themselves, and we keep no metadata. We take privacy seriously."

JPD: "As any *Shark Tank* viewer knows, you don't invest in average businesses. Why do you feel this is a great business?"

MC: "This is a great business because being able to minimize our digital footprint is critical when a single out-of-context social media post can ruin a career or even be far worse."

JPD: "Why do you believe customers will come to Cyber Dust? Are we craving privacy? Are we afraid we might make an online mistake that will haunt us later? Are we just becoming more paranoid?"

MC: "There is zero upside to letting your digital footprint expand. It's not so much that we crave privacy but that we all know or have read about someone who has been burned on social media. We have taught our kids not to post pictures publicly that could impact their future, but we have not yet taught ourselves that texts, messages, and social media posts could be used just as maliciously or with as much downside as pictures.

"As far as Cyber Dust as a product, we do far more than just protect your messages. We see it used as a productivity tool:

By pushing messages with Cyber Dust, you eliminate much of the procrastination of e-mail. When you open a Cyber Dust message, you have to respond while the message is fresh in your mind. No more e-mail getting bottled up in your inbox.

"Our blast feature is being used by companies, celebrities, and experts as a private alternative to Twitter. I can send a company-wide update, distribute motivational quotes, or ask questions to a group, and any follow-up is absolutely private. And unlike Twitter, there are no trolls."

JPD: "You've been quoted suggesting that your own legal cases motivated you to create the app, saying that in one case, Securities and Exchange Commission lawyers took every digital message you gave them and applied whatever context that they wanted to apply. What do you think of the accusation by lawyers who say you have devised Cyber Dust as a way to avoid legal discovery?"

MC: "They are correct. It is intentional. If we are alone and talk face-to-face, we avoid discovery. Cyber Dust is the digital equivalent to a face-to-face conversation."

JPD: "What do you think the future holds for online privacy? Will texting with services like Cyber Dust and your competitors become the norm? Will we look for ways to use tech less?"

MC: "I'm not sure, but I think we'll be very careful about who can see what we send or post. The bottom line is this: When you hit send on a text or tweet, you lose ownership of it—but you don't lose responsibility. Every text you have sent may have been saved and could be out there waiting to be used in ways you didn't imagine. Even the most simple of posts can be used out of context, often unintentionally, and change your future."

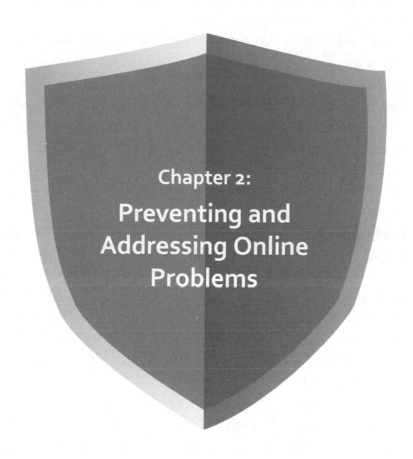

Chapter 2:

Preventing and Addressing Online Problems

A young man reached out to me with a story that's emblematic of what this book is all about. He did something incredibly stupid that had been memorialized online, and he wanted to have this information removed from the internet. Yet upon further review, he hasn't really learned his lesson and is likely in for an incredibly harsh reality check, even though it is hard to imagine things getting worse.

This wayward soul did something that many 21-year-olds do: He went out one night and got terrifically drunk. Sure, many of us have had one too many and embarrassed ourselves. Some would call it a rite of passage. Our guy, whom I will call Kevin, took it to another level.

Police were anonymously called, and they found Kevin, lying in his own urine-soaked clothing, passed out in his car. Fearing for his safety, they took him to a hospital where an emergency room doctor determined his blood alcohol level (BAC) was above .40. In most states, .08 BAC is legally drunk. On one chart I saw, a reading of .37 BAC indicated that "death is possible." And nearly all individuals who reach .45 BAC die.[1]

Kevin was placed in a room to hopefully sleep it off while the cops tried to track down his parents. He wasn't a good patient. He repeatedly tried to remove IV tubes that were hydrating him, and he was belligerent to the hospital staff. Then he walked out of the hospital and was arrested for drunk and disorderly conduct as well as indecent exposure, because he was still wearing the hospital gown. You know the type—the gown ties in the back so you are, indeed, indecently exposed.

News of Kevin's escapades appeared on dozens of news websites, including one of the highest authority news sites on the planet. I'm not trying to pile on here. Frankly, his story, though wild and wacky, wouldn't have even made it into this book had it not been for what happened when I further looked into his background.

He reached out to me more than two years after this incident because he was having trouble finding a job. He wasn't particularly good at returning my phone calls, so I decided to do some additional digging. I looked at his Facebook page and saw photo after photo of Kevin drinking, including one picture of him in front of a sign that read, "Let's drink until we can't feel feelings anymore."

Even though Kevin had gone through this major ordeal, he hadn't learned from it, and it was easy to see why he wasn't finding work. His privacy settings were wide open on Facebook so that anyone—meaning I or a human resources person—could very quickly see that Kevin still liked to tip one back. And that's assuming he could get past the first level of researching done by a recruiter and somehow explain away his .40 night. The message is this: You have to *want* to protect yourself online.

Preventive Measures

The best way to have a solid online reputation is to have a solid offline reputation. If you can keep your nose clean, then you are many times less likely to have a problem. We can prevent a lot of problems by following the many golden rules we learned from our parents:

- Do unto others as you would have them do unto you.
- Neither a borrower nor a lender be.
- Don't drink and drive, or drive and text.
- Don't tug on Superman's cape.
- Nothing good happens in a strip club after midnight.
- Be careful of what you post and keep your privacy settings up to date.

Do you leave the door to your house wide open? Would you leave your car unlocked with the keys in it on a busy urban street? Would you walk around naked in public? Of course not. Yet many people do the digital equivalent when they open up their online lives to the general public.

If you would be embarrassed about seeing your personal business posted on the front page of the *New York Times*, then you shouldn't post it online. Of course, the editors at the *Times* don't care that you love the new restaurant that you discovered or that your kid made the honor roll. They also won't put details of your night of drunken debauchery in their pages, but you still wouldn't want to see it there.

Without mounting a massive moral high horse, it's difficult to tell people how to lead their lives and what should and shouldn't be shared. On the whole, we should all think about any posts that might be controversial and realize that things can be forwarded and shared by others very quickly.

Know Who Your Friends Are

As I sit finalizing the first draft of this book, it is late April 2016, and the talk of the town in southern Florida is the online saga of football player Laremy Tunsil, the first round draft pick of the Miami Dolphins. Tunsil was slated to be a top draft choice by the NFL, but just 13 minutes before the draft started, a photo was posted on Tunsil's Twitter account showing him apparently smoking marijuana. Tunsil, who some experts said was the best player in the draft, dropped 13 places, and some are speculating that his fall will cost him millions of dollars.

While I know that Tunsil's plight will not be the last social media gaffe to make national news, it does serve as a yet another reminder of the perils of social media use among young people—the controversial photo of Tunsil was allegedly taken years ago when he was still in high school. I discussed the situation with my 16-year-old daughter and my 14-year-old son, both of whom spend a great deal of time communicating on their mobile devices and using social media. As parents are prone to do, I attempted to pass along to my kids some advice gleaned from not only my experience writing this book but also from life. My hope is that these lessons will be of value to my kids and maybe the young people in your life too.

Part of Tunsil's problem was that the video of him smoking pot, wearing a gas mask nonetheless, found its way into the hands of someone he couldn't trust. Allegedly, he was blackmailed. The lesson is this: Know who your friends are and stay together. A friend doesn't encourage you to do something illegal, a friend doesn't ask you to hack into someone's phone, and a friend doesn't blackmail you on Twitter. Keep your friends close and distance yourself from your enemies. Just as you don't consider every person whom you meet to be your actual friend, so should you not invite everyone you meet online to be your friend online.

Privacy settings can be confusing—but they're key to your online reputation. I follow a few rules for social media sites. On Twitter, I have open settings and post general things about my life and business. I will let anyone follow me, but I don't immediately follow back anyone who follows me. A few years ago, I learned of a tourism bureau that had set up its Twitter account to automatically follow back anyone who followed the bureau. Makes sense, right? If someone is following you, then they likely have an interest in you, your business, or, in this case, the destination. Unfortunately, one of the bureau's followers turned out to be an escort service, which was then automatically followed back by the tourism bureau. Oops.

On LinkedIn, a person needs to be a connection in order to see beyond my basic profile, and this is the default setting. If I have met someone in a business setting, I will likely accept their invitation to connect and often reach out to people in this circumstance and connect. I rarely accept invitations to connect from people whom I haven't met, though I know many people who do, as they like to increase their sheer volume of connections. If there is someone I want to meet on LinkedIn, I may try to connect with them, but I'm not bothered if they ignore me. While I use most of the default settings on LinkedIn, I have closed off my list of connections. My business network is valuable, and you don't get to see it just because we are buddies on the social media site.

If you are apt to make deep emotional statements on Facebook, it's best to not include your work colleagues within your Facebook sphere. If you are very political, which is fine by the way, then it's probably best not to include in your network those people who may vehemently disagree with you. On my personal Facebook account (as opposed to a public, searchable page), I post more details about my personal life, my political views, my sports fandom, and my family. On Facebook, I decided that I would only connect with people whom I have met "in the flesh" and with whom I am comfortable sharing my personal info. This may be more restrictive than what others believe, but it works for me. I'm comfortable with my Facebook network being this size, and it enables me to communicate without any major restrictions. People who know me understand my sense of humor, quirks, and beliefs. Go Gators.

If we go back to the Justine Sacco case and her tweet heard 'round the world, we can learn some lessons.

Digital is fast. Sacco's plight may have staying power among social media historians as an example of how quickly information can move around the globe. One tweet by a person with a few hundred followers can spread across the internet in a matter of hours and turn into a national news story. Sacco's tweet was covered by many major news outlets, and she went from unknown to famous to infamous in less than a day.

Digital is forever. We already know we need to be careful about what we post online because what's online can stay there for decades. Copies are made quickly online, and we can no longer "burn the negatives" of images we wish to destroy forever. This time, though, the lesson comes not from a photo taken in a fraternity house by a 20-something but rather an experienced business professional who absolutely should have known better.

Murphy was right. Part of what made the Sacco episode a phenomenon was the confluence of events that proved Murphy's law: Anything that can go wrong will go wrong. Sacco wrote an offensive tweet and then got on an airplane. While in the air, the tweet caught viral fire, but the author was completely unaware of the conflagration. The fact that she was airborne and out of touch actually fed the mob, as people speculated what would happen when she touched down and checked her e-mail. As Sacco cruised high in the sky, the impact began to grow exponentially. It's a truth-is-stranger-than-fiction scenario that should impart a lesson to all of us that we have to remain vigilant about what we post, because there's always a chance it could go wickedly wrong.

It's hard to tell ha-ha funny from weird funny. My guess is that Sacco was trying to be funny with her tweet. The "just kidding" line is a dead giveaway. I'm sure even she can't explain how it was humorous, but the larger point is that sometimes it is best to leave being funny to comedians. It's one thing to be funny among one's own circle of friends but completely another to be funny to the masses. And successfully conveying humor in 140 characters is no easy task. Attempting humor about something as terrible as AIDS should be avoided in the same way we don't discuss sex, politics, or religion at cocktail parties. Sadly for Sacco, her attempt at a joke left no one laughing, except for a sarcastic few within the mob, which was certainly not her intended audience.

Take Control of Your Online Reputation

Some people still say that they "don't do social media" and that they steer clear of that "silly stuff." And statistics support this; according to Pew Research Center, as of July 2015, more than 15 percent of Americans still don't use the internet.[2] While it seems shocking to those of us who live and breathe marketing, millions of folks continue to have no interest in social media channels. While ignorance is bliss, it's not smart online behavior.

One reason is chaos theory—or at least chaos theory as I remember it explained in the novel and movie *Jurassic Park*. As you may recall from the story, the ecosystem created on the island for the dinosaurs was so complicated and nonlinear that its future couldn't be accurately predicted. They tried to suppress the dinosaur's instinct to reproduce, but nature found a way. Chaos ruled.

Imagine that the internet is now nature and it has a new kind of T. rex. You can't hide your image from it. The internet will find a way.

If someone is looking for information about you, they will find it online—I promise. Everyone has left digital bread crumbs somewhere. The internet may find benign things like property listings, old newspaper clippings, or corporate filings. But it can also find less benign things like arrest reports, lawsuits, and negative reviews and blog posts. If you don't take control of your online reputation, then someone else will—your customers, your competitors, or, worst case, no one (a.k.a. chaos). Ignore your digital image at your own peril.

Here are a few simple things you can do to protect your online reputation.

Build your social profile. Ultimately, when people are checking you out online, they want to find the most relevant information. Take control of your online profile by populating the internet with positive information. Here are four quick ways to take control of your search results:

1. Create your own website (try to get your name as the URL) and post your resume there.

2. Get a LinkedIn account with your photo, current education, and job history posted.

3. Create a Twitter account with your name in it, and post business-related content.

4. Secure a Facebook page with your real name and complete your profile. Unlike regular Facebook accounts that are closed to Google searches, Facebook Pages (the company capitalizes the term) are public and searchable.

Just doing these four things can fairly quickly give you control of 40 percent of the first page of Google results for your name. This will help identify you on the web because these sites have tremendous authority with search engines. Google, Bing, and Yahoo give greater weight to sites with high authority. This will help people who are looking for you to find the real you instead of a namesake or a competitor. And you will have staked a virtual claim on what can become valuable digital real estate.

Google yourself every once in a while. See how you are perceived by the most powerful digital front door so you can react if something goes wrong or something weird happens.

The unrelated namesake of a client once committed a silly, foolish crime that was all over the internet. When someone Googled our client's name, they saw links to stories about the foolish guy. While most people knew that our client wasn't the fool, the crazy story made it harder for potential customers to find him. We fixed it by boosting our client's social and digital profile. The foolish guy stories didn't go away, but our client's links moved up the rankings.

Whether we like it or not, the digital world is a powerful force in defining our public persona. It's best to address it now and prevent potential chaos.

Don't feel compelled to document everything with photos and videos. For most teens, the mobile phone is like an extra appendage, and the urge is strong to document every occurrence with photo or video evidence. It is with the wisdom of experience that I explain that a day will come when they will do something embarrassing. I know, I did plenty in my youth, and I thank the technology gods, for my sake and that of my friends, that cell phone cameras were not around when I lived in a fraternity house. All of our kids will have bad moments, so let's remind them not to memorialize these moments on the internet. All things don't merit digital documentation.

Follow the rules. Tunsil's first mistake was smoking weed. It's illegal for anyone under the age of 21 to smoke marijuana in the United States. You may not agree with it, but it's the law. The same is true for drinking. Though more socially acceptable, it's still illegal everywhere for kids to drink.

Respect one another and respect yourself. If your boyfriend or girlfriend wants to make a sex tape, stop. If your boyfriend asks you to send a naked selfie, stop. If your girlfriend wants to send you a topless photo, say no. Girls need to stop taking naked pictures of themselves, and boys need to stop asking. Tunsil put himself at risk when he broke the rules and the publisher of the photo exploited the football player's vulnerability. Neither person in this equation showed much self-respect. If you respect yourself, then by default, you will respect others.

When it comes to job searches, there are other things you can do:

Be proactive, not reactive. Prospective employers will likely Google your name and see what comes up. Cleaning up your online reputation begins with seeing if it needs to be cleaned up in the first place.

Control your content. This might seem obvious, but don't post anything you don't want your mother, employer, or potential clients to see. Delete or untag any embarrassing or inappropriate pictures and posts. The last thing you would want is a drunken night from years ago costing you a chance to land your first job. Even after you land your first job out of college, you shouldn't forget about your online reputation.

Make Your Mobile Phone Valueless

Saying "valueless" may sound strange, but there's a very good reason. Since I started helping people with online reputation issues, I have heard some amazing tales, but few are as educational as this one. A lady called me up with an awful problem. Her phone had been stolen from her locker at her job, and within hours—yes, you may have already guessed it—inappropriate and embarrassing pictures of her were available for everyone to see on the internet.

She had made three mistakes, all preventable.

1. First, there's the idea of taking naked pictures of oneself. Duh! This one confounds me but it persists in our society. Perhaps it's because celebrities are handsomely rewarded

for posting naked pictures of themselves online and also because young people tend to be too trusting of technology. Whatever the motivation, we need to teach our sons and daughters not to do this and also teach them not to ask it of other people.

2. This young lady didn't enable the passcode feature on her phone.

3. She didn't set up the Find My iPhone or remote data-erasing features.

In her case, three strikes equaled revenge porn. Sadly, we can purchase protection to replace a lost or stolen phone, but no such insurance exists for a damaged reputation.

Aside from the embarrassing content that may be on the phone itself, if you truly want to protect yourself from the many perils of a lost or stolen phone, you need to have everything of value backed up, preferably automatically. If you lose possession of your phone, the physical value of your phone should be the only concern you have. Here's how you do it—and the cloud service providers are going to love me for saying this.

E-mail. Many of us transact most of our business through e-mail, and we would be lost if a month's or even a few days' worth of e-mails were permanently lost. Prevent this by using an e-mail platform that saves all of your e-mails in the cloud, such as a virtual exchange server or even Gmail, which enables you to check e-mail from multiple devices. When using this type of service, if you change your password and/or wipe your phone, then no one can access your e-mail except you.

Pictures and music. Photos document life's moments, and you certainly don't want to lose your memories if your phone ends up in the ocean (or a pitcher of margaritas, but that's another story). The same is true for your music. Set up your phone to automatically back up to the cloud so you have copies without even thinking about it.

Notes and other stuff. If you take a lot of notes on your phone, make sure they are backed up or use one of the cloud-based note services like Evernote. If your phone disappears, then all you need to do is change your password and your notes are safe.

Set up the passcode on your phone. I will admit that I didn't use this feature initially on my iPhone, but now it is a necessity. It requires you to enter a four-digit code to access your phone. You can set it so that it is required each time you open it or after your phone has been idle for a set amount of time, up to one hour. There are ten thousand possible codes, so it is not easily hacked, unless you choose the lazy path and use a really dumb passcode like "1234," "0000," or your birth year. Use a passcode and make it unique.

Be prepared to wipe. This is the heart of the "make it valueless" proposition. Essentially, you should be prepared to wipe your phone of all its information at any time. All of your data and anything important should be backed up to the cloud so that if your phone is lost or stolen, your information won't be compromised. Both Apple and Android phones offer this, but you have to set it up. In addition, I recommend that you enable the setting on your iPhone to automatically wipe it if the passcode is entered incorrectly after 10 attempts.

Yes, I know that you may forget your code or one of your friends may mess with you and accidentally wipe your phone, but more than likely this feature could help you more than it could harm you. It's much easier to deal with a lost phone than lost personal data.

And here's one more suggestion that some would say is heresy: Get rid of your smartphone and get an old-fashioned flip phone. They're cheap, durable, have a long battery life, and they're not connected to the web. Hackers work to collect phone information, and there are many incidents of rogue apps and other attacks on smartphones. Flip phones generally don't store or have the ability to share personal information aside from a few photos and your archive of texts, which you can periodically delete.

What to Do if It Happens to You

Let's say that despite all of my warnings, horror stories, and preventive advice, you become a victim of an online attack. What can you do about it? As we've discussed, each situation is different, and the solutions vary too. In some situations, a legal solution might be in order. In others, it may make sense to try to negotiate removal. The most popular option is to suppress the negative search result. And in still other instances, covert ops solutions may be in order, and I'll discuss those later in this chapter.

Hate blogs and hate websites can pop up overnight, and if written by clever authors, they can quickly rise to the top of search results. Reputational and economic damage frequently follow.

When confronted with negative online content that hinders your business or damages your reputation, the best advice is to remain calm and make a sound assessment. While the first reaction may be to blast away at the hate blog, defamatory post, negative news article, or nasty review, we have found that it makes more sense to slow down and develop a strategy before confronting the source— assuming you can figure out who posted the negative information in the first place.

First, do no harm. Every complex online reputation issue is a little bit different. Some site owners, when confronted, will comply with requests for removal while others will stand firm. Some have developed processes to handle removal requests and will only follow their own in-house procedures. Make sure that, whatever your first step is, you don't make the situation worse.

You have the right to remain silent. Though silence can be a big mistake when dealing with a traditional public relations crisis, with online issues it can be a prudent strategy. An impetuous response to the negative search result may add credibility to untrue allegations and fuel the fire of a renegade blogger. If your business receives a negative review, a response may be warranted, but in most cases, silence is a good first step.

Can it be removed? Contrary to popular belief, you can remove negative Google search results. It's not always possible, but there are situations when it can be done.

Determine if you want to develop a legal strategy, removal strategy, or suppression strategy. Review your options and then move forward. Do it quickly, but not in a hurry.

Hiring a Lawyer

When I speak to people about online problems, I almost always get legal questions. "Can't I just hire a lawyer?" "What about the police?" "Isn't the law on my side to get things removed from the internet?"

If someone has been victimized (theft, fraud, privacy invasion, or identity theft), or they feel threatened in any way, then my advice is to contact the police and/or a lawyer. In some situations, a legal approach may be the best way to go, and I would never recommend against speaking with a lawyer about an online problem. I will discuss defamation in detail in this chapter and review what several attorneys have told me about these types of situations. But if you want legal advice, speak to a lawyer, and I can recommend a few.

The truth is that the majority of online attacks do not involve defamation. And proving defamation is difficult while collecting damages in a defamation case is even tougher.

Here's the reality of it all: If someone says something negative about you or your business online, it probably isn't against the law. It may be a matter of opinion, as written on a review site. It may be negative but posted by someone anonymously. Or it may be true, but you just don't like seeing it online. None of these things is illegal. Yes, they are mean and can be damaging to you and your business, but the perpetrator likely didn't break any laws.

And even if a law were broken, it is very difficult technologically to get to the bottom of online attacks. Yes, the FBI and law enforcement agencies can figure out which computers are used for cyber-attacks and the like, but the reality is that neither the FBI nor any concerned citizen want to divert federal law enforcement resources away from identifying truly bad guys, like domestic terrorists, to instead figuring out who wrote a bunch of nasty reviews about your franchise restaurant. Law enforcement has better things to do. Unfortunate, but true.

Again, if you are being harassed online, cyberstalked, or feel threatened due to someone's actions online, call the police. It's why we pay taxes and a benefit of living in a civilized society.

And there's another important economic reality. Lawyers need to get paid in order to assist you, and most lawyers are compensated on an hourly basis. So just to speak with you about your case, it's likely that an attorney will want to be paid. Some lawyers will take cases on a contingency basis, so they get paid a percentage of monetary damages awarded to a victim by a court. Such cases are very complicated, and whether or not an attorney will represent you on a contingency basis has as much to do with who you are suing as the details of the case itself.

I will repeat: I don't have anything against lawyers. (My father and both of my brothers are lawyers, and I'm friends with dozens of attorneys.) One just has to understand the economic factors that impact involving an attorney in an online reputation issue.

Attorneys who I know who handle defamation cases will reiterate that just having a conversation with a lawyer about your case will likely cost hundreds of dollars, as that's what most attorneys in this field charge on an hourly basis. If after an initial consultation a victim of an online problem is willing to pay what will likely be thousands of dollars in legal fees, then I say go for it.

Now, if you happen to have been defamed online by a large corporation with insurance against such things, or by a conspicuously wealthy person, then an attorney may take your case on a contingency basis. Perhaps there's a payday in your future, but in most instances, it's not a reasonable option.

If a web posting is truly defamatory, then it can be removed, but you are going to need legal counsel. I have pulled together some basic information on defamation, culled from my experience with journalism and media law. Defamatory blog posts can be taken down. It just takes some work.

Defamation, simply put, is a catch-all term for any statement that is knowingly false and intended to hurt someone's reputation. It is further subdivided into libel (written defamation) and slander (spoken defamation). Because of the infinite memory of the internet, defamatory statements that are posted online often have a significant shelf life, which can have a long-term negative effect on the individual or business mentioned.

If you feel you need to take legal action, there are steps that can be taken to remedy the situation. Successfully trying an online defamation case can prove difficult, but it can be done.

If the content you want removed is something negative about you or your business, this type of item usually cannot be removed without legal documentation supporting your claims. Under Section 230 of the U.S. Communications Decency Act of 1996 (CDA), hosting companies and websites are under no legal obligation to remove allegedly defamatory content without a court's determination that the content is knowingly false and harmful towards you or your business.

For example, if you have a bad experience at a restaurant, you have the right to go online and write a negative review about that restaurant. Although the owner of the restaurant may not like it, you are allowed to express your opinion. However, you cannot go online and write that your waiter is a pedophile just to get back at him for dropping a plate of pasta in your lap. The bad review is not defamatory, but calling the waiter a pedophile is.

In order to prove that something is defamatory, four elements must be met:

1. There is a false statement of fact.
2. The false statement has been publicly published, and at least one other person has seen it.
3. The false statement was published with some level of fault.
4. The false statement must have caused damage to the talked-about person's reputation.

So if you find a negative item online and it meets all four points to qualify as defamatory, you should contact an attorney who specializes in internet defamation.

Providing the legal documentation stating that the content you want removed is defamatory enables websites and hosting companies to assist you. If served with a court order stating that the item in question is defamatory, they will very likely take it down. Remember that the bar of proof of defamation can be high.

Here's just one example. In 2011, a widely distributed anonymous e-mail message attacked Sandals, the operator of luxury, all-inclusive resorts in the Caribbean. The message implied that Sandals used racist hiring policies that discriminated against local Jamaicans, who were given menial service jobs at the resort while foreigners got high-paying executive jobs. Sandals sought disclosure of information and materials that would enable it to bring a libel claim against the holder of the Google Gmail account from which the offending e-mail was sent. In order to receive this information, Sandals was required to demonstrate that its libel claim against the anonymous writer had merit. Because the allegedly defamatory statements were deemed by the court to be *nonactionable opinion*, the court denied Sandals' request for the identifying information. In its judgment rendered on May 19, 2011, the Supreme Court, Appellate Division, First Department, New York found that the e-mail was nonactionable opinion because it "does not contain assertions of fact, nor would a reasonable person construe that it does." The court continued: "For the most part, the account holder enumerates queries in response to articles and pictures. The account holder provides links to the text on which his/her assertions are based." These links, according to the court, provided the reader with the facts and allowed the reader to arrive at his or her own conclusions, indicating to the reader "that the account holder's words are meant to provoke either thought or discussion and are therefore protected speech." The court also found that the resort company "offer[ed] no evidence of the harm the account holder's e-mail has caused it" and therefore could not satisfy the "injury" element of a libel cause of action.[3]

Another downside to taking legal action is that information is added to the public record—which can then be accessed by anyone and published online without issue. Raanan Katz, a shopping center developer and minority owner of the Miami Heat professional basketball team, was engaged in a contentious battle with blogger Irina Chevaldina. While the subject of the fight was small potatoes by journalistic standards, Chevaldina took one action that really ticked off Katz. On her blog, she published an unflattering photo of Katz, taken while he was courtside at a basketball game. In the picture, Katz is looking askance and his tongue is sticking out of the side of his mouth—the image has some Jabba the Hutt qualities if you ask me.

In what I'm sure his lawyers thought was a cleaver move, Katz went heavy on the legal side and secured the copyright to the photo. He then promptly sued Chevaldina for copyright infringement, intending to force the blogger to take down the photo.

The court of public opinion (and the Court of Appeals for the Eleventh Circuit) thought otherwise. Free speech groups came to Chevaldina's defense and a number of reporters were notified. When the court ruled in the blogger's favor, news spread fast and so did the picture, which has now been republished by dozens of news sites. The image that Katz clearly dislikes has now reached a far greater audience than had he not made the argument public through legal filings.

Violations of Terms and Conditions on Blogging Platforms

Blogging platforms such as WordPress are notoriously protective of their user's freedom of speech and allow them to freely express their ideas and opinions without censoring them. They will not suspend blogs if they are not in violation of their terms of service, even if they are posting content that is offensive or objectionable. However, they do take their terms of service seriously and will suspend any sites that are found to be in violation. Blog posts that violate terms of service can be removed.

Here is what the majority of blog platforms do *not* allow their users to post:

- adult content
- exploitation of children
- hate speech
- crude content
- harassment
- copyright infringement
- personal and confidential information
- impersonation of others

If you find that the content falls under any of the categories listed above, we suggest that you report it to the blog platform. It will take your report under consideration and may remove the content or send the user a warning.

Because popular blogging sites offer a wide range of customization options, it's sometimes difficult to tell which, if any, blogging platform is being used by the author. You can find out by looking at the source code. This may sound difficult, but it really isn't. The easiest way to find the source code is to use the keyboard shortcut Ctrl+U (Windows, Linux) or Command+U (Mac). You will see a bunch of HTML code, and usually near the top of the page you will see clues as to which blogging platform is being used.

If you do a search and find the word "blogspot," the blog is hosted by Blogger, which is owned by Google. If you search the code and find "tumblr," then you know you are dealing with a Tumblr blog. If you search and find the term "wp-theme," then it is most likely a WordPress blog.

Different blog platforms offer different ways of reporting content that is negative or abusive. Listed below are links to the terms of service and how to report content for the three major blog platforms:

Blogger

- Terms of service: *www.blogger.com/content.g*
- How to report content: to report content on Blogger, visit *http://support.google.com/blogger/answer/76315?hl=en* and select the abuse type to access the relevant contact form

Tumblr

- Terms of service: *www.tumblr.com/policy/en/terms_of_service*
- How to report content: e-mail abuse@tumblr.com

Word Press

- Terms of service: *http://en.wordpress.com/tos*
- How to report content: for logged-in WordPress users to report content, use the "report this content button" located underneath the blog menu on the toolbar. If you are not a logged-in WordPress user, you can use the form found here: *http://en.wordpress.com/abuse*

While proving defamation may be difficult, having a lawyer help you is often a smart move. If you are dealing with negative content on a website run by a reputable organization, then a strongly worded letter from an attorney may be sufficiently intimidating to a business that they will take down negative content. Most businesses don't welcome legal troubles, and having a lawyer write a letter on your behalf may be a good early move when trying to get negative content taken down. While government sites, top-tier news sites, or complaint sites won't blink, others may prefer to remove the negative item rather than risk a lawsuit. Just as you have to hire a lawyer to file a lawsuit, a company has to hire one to defend it at a cost of hundreds of dollars per hour.

Negotiate, Beg, and Plead

Most websites are run by legitimate businesses that have no interest in publishing false, tasteless, or potentially defamatory content. Of course, some sites are run by neurotic bloggers, but the vast majority have sensible human beings at the controls. If you are dealing with negative web postings or negative articles posted on a corporate site or corporate message board, it may be possible to negotiate removal. We have had instances where individuals not affiliated with a company-sponsored message board posted negative information about our clients. We contacted the company and asked them to take it down, and the negative post was quickly removed. We explained to the company that the comment or posting was in bad taste and potentially defamatory and that it didn't match with the company's brand and image.

The website owner may be unaware of the type of content that is being published on their site and might be surprised to learn of inappropriate content. On several occasions, we have contacted websites hosting negative posts and negotiated for removal. With the right approach, it often works. Once the content is removed from the site, it will eventually fall from Google search results. Sometimes it helps to have a third party make the request on your behalf.

Most people who reach out to me have already tried this in some manner. They have contacted a website directly or the local newspaper that published an article about them. Some websites may comply but others will not. This is a strategy that will *not* work when talking to a government agency, a major news outlet, review site, complaint site, or any site that makes money from having negative info published.

It is worth the effort because the payoff can be rich, as many websites have no interest in being purveyors of salacious or negative information. If you are a sympathetic character, you may have a better chance of finding the right sort of person to make the change on your behalf. It's definitely a viable strategy that takes some time, work, and research, but it can pay off.

Case Study: Hunting Guide Company

One of my first online reputation management clients was a company in the hunting guide industry. A disgruntled customer wrote a negative review on an industry forum, complaining that the company's services were inadequate and a rip-off and that—here's the kicker—one of the employees (who was singled out by name) was on drugs. This particular entry was posted on a prominent industry website, and when you Googled the topic or the company, the negative posting appeared on page one of search results.

The owner of the company was very upset about the posting for a number of reasons. His was a leading company in its industry and, aside from this one angry customer, had an excellent reputation. He knew who the customer was and had made efforts to "make the situation right" by offering a partial refund and other amends. The executive was offended by the posting because he believed it was not only untrue but also defamatory to one of his employees. Finally, he crunched the numbers and determined that this negative review had already cost him about $80,000 in revenue. He was highly motivated to get this negative post removed.

We analyzed the situation and learned that the website hosting the forum post was run by an up-and-coming, progressive media company that, in my opinion, was trying to build its own reputation in the client's industry. We reached out to them with a fairly simple message: We wanted them to remove the post because it was potentially defamatory. Though I'm not a lawyer, I do know that you can't name someone online and say they are on drugs unless they had been arrested or convicted of possession, or perhaps living in Colorado. We also stressed that this type of post was clearly not in the spirit and mission of the aspiring media company. We held back on any confrontational language or legal threats. First it's best to try a little honey.

Determining who to contact can be a challenge, but in this case we were able to get our request in the hands of the right person. They responded quickly, and the post was taken down in less than 24 hours. We reported the dead link to Google and it was gone from search results within a few days. Mission accomplished.

The Suppression Game

When you research online reputation management websites (the best-known example is Reputation.com), you quickly learn that they offer a distinct service known in the industry as suppression. Reputation.com and other similar companies will create new, benign web content with the hopes of pushing down or suppressing negative search results. This tactic can be very effective, but it isn't always the best solution or the most economical—though the prices are dropping.

The idea is that you flood the internet with positive content about you or your company and work to push down, bury, or suppress the negative content. Information is not removed from search results but rather pushed farther down the search result pages to a point where fewer people will see it.

When individuals search for information online, they rarely go past the first few pages of search results, so if a negative item is, for example, on page three or beyond, only a fraction of folks looking online will see it. A number of studies have been completed regarding this, and while the methodologies are different and the results vary, I can confidently tell you that the majority of people looking for information don't get past page three. A study published on the Marketing Land website in 2014 suggests that the first five listings *on page one alone* get more than 65 percent of clicks.[4]

In addition, there's a psychological benefit from having a negative item appear low on the search results. The implication to the reader is that because it's low, it's less important than the items above it.

I will leave the exact numbers to the search engine optimization experts, but it is absolutely true that you can bury negative results. It can be an effective strategy. The problem lies with the fact that when someone is really checking you out—for a job, for a consulting contract, to remodel their home, or to see if you are good enough for their only daughter—they will look past page one and maybe even past page 100.

Today, there are hundreds of companies that offer online reputation management services. For many, even those within the tech industry, the terms "online reputation management" and "suppression" are the same thing. This industry has grown in the past several years, and its start is most frequently traced to Reputation.com. I don't know if Reputation.com invented suppression, but it was the first company to offer suppression on a large scale and the first to market it.

Many public relations firms and most search engine optimization companies will say that they offer online reputation services in some regard. In my experience, 99 percent of these companies are offering suppression services. The other tactics that I suggest aren't even on the radar of most companies within the online reputation management marketplace. In fact, if you call Reputation.com or most of the companies that advertise these services, you will be told that they will make no efforts to *remove* negative content. While it may sound like I'm bashing Reputation.com, that's not the case. The executives at that company have created a systematic and scalable approach to dealing with online problems. As far as I can tell, it's a successful company that dominates its industry. I have used suppression tactics to help my clients, but I also believe other options can be more effective.

The companies that offer suppression services will charge anywhere from a few hundred to tens of thousands of dollars to create new online content that will appear on the search engines ahead of negative posts. A typical online reputation management company will look at your situation and likely suggest a package of services that it hopes will suppress or push down the negative results. It does this by using some of the tactics that I mentioned earlier.

For example, it creates accounts for you on Facebook, Twitter, LinkedIn, Pinterest, Google+, YouTube, Vimeo, and dozens of other high authority public websites. It will then work with you to create new content for these sites, such as daily or weekly posts, photos, and videos. It will create all manners of digital assets on your behalf and then optimize them so that they appear high on search results.

This may include creating blog sites and microsites on your behalf and also generating new content to populate the many new pages. And the strategy works in some cases, as negative information is pushed from page one, and the client is happy that the negative content is only found in the most definitive of searches.

In some instances, the negative stories can't be pushed down. Some suppression tactics may work in the short term, but as the search engines adjust their parameters, search results can change. We have seen situations where people have embarked on a suppression strategy only to find that six months out, after paying thousands of dollars on an ongoing basis, they have the same problem or find themselves going backward after Google makes changes to its search algorithm.

Another issue that I have with suppression is that you are trying to game the system. Is it a viable long-term strategy to try to outsmart the engineers at Google, Yahoo, and Bing? Google is a multi-billion-dollar company and has some of the brightest people in the world working for it. Google's goal as a search company is to offer people the best possible and most authentic information on what they are searching for. If I have to bet on whether a suppression strategy will work long term versus the goals of the engineers at Google, I pick the wonks.

In the end, it comes down to *authority*. Information on major news sites, government websites, and high profile social media sites may outperform all the content created with a suppression campaign. I have spoken with dozens of people who have been trying to suppress negative content for years. But the reality is that a story on a major news outlet or a press release about a government investigation sometimes will not be suppressed, even by the companies that virtually invented the push down and bury tactics.

One of the overall positives of suppression is that you can do some of the work yourself. Using the high authority social media sites and a few other tricks can be very effective. And sometimes, it's the only option.

Case Study: Julian

Julian was facing a tough predicament. After being arrested for allegedly soliciting an escort, the police distributed a news release that listed his name among dozens of others charged during the anti-prostitution sting operation.

A technology consultant who needed to regularly secure new engagements, Julian's online reputation was directly tied to his ability to earn a living. He contacted me a few weeks after the arrest, and the news was already impacting him both personally and professionally. His family was embarrassed, and he believed his future contracts were in jeopardy.

When you searched his name on Google, nearly half of the first page of results mentioned the police sting, and he was clearly associated with the misdeed. Because the news was reported on several news sites, including that of a major metropolitan daily newspaper, I knew that it would be difficult to negotiate direct removal of the results. High authority sites like major newspapers are also outside the realm of even the expensive covert ops guys. We decided on suppression and mounted a campaign to flood the internet with positive information about Julian that would push down the negative news.

First, we tackled the major social media sites, ensuring that Julian had complete profiles on Facebook, Twitter, LinkedIn, and Google+. Search engines like Google, Yahoo, and Bing view sites like these as high-authority providers of information, and they typically dominate the first pages of search results for individuals.

Next we created a vanity site for Julian, purchasing his full name as the URL and populating the site with business and personal information. Remember that Google and the other search engines want to send users to the best possible sources regarding a search term, so claiming Julian's full name as a website URL, and then adding real information about him, created a strong digital asset. In addition, we created other digital content on Julian's behalf, including videos, which were posted on sites like YouTube and Vimeo, and images posted on sites like Pinterest.

Over the next several weeks and months, we consistently posted new information to his social media sites, his vanity site, and to other places on the web. Julian began to see results within the first month of our suppression campaign as his Facebook, Twitter, and LinkedIn accounts worked their way up page one of search results, which in turn started to push down the negative stories.

It took some time, about three months in total, but we eventually gained control of 90 percent of the search results for his name on the first page of Google results, and we eliminated any mention of his arrest when you searched the first four pages of results on both Yahoo and Bing. As of this writing, while anyone who is truly digging for dirt on Julian will be able to find information about his arrest, the casual web surfer is more likely to find positive or benign content about him.

The results we secured for Julian are fairly typical of a suppression campaign. We didn't eliminate any negative content, but we were able to push it down to pages that most folks never reach. We weren't able to completely clean up his online results, but we improved his online profile enough that he continues to get new job assignments and can lead his life as a productive citizen.

Julian entered a pre-trial intervention agreement regarding his arrest. The case was eventually dismissed and his criminal record expunged.

Covert Ops

One of the internet's big secrets is that digital is not necessarily forever. The common belief is that once something is posted online, it will stay there forever. Many people endure a feeling of helplessness at this thought, but options exist. Content can actually be removed from search results and sometimes entirely from cyberspace. I'm not saying it's easy or that removal practices are prevalent, but it can be done.

Sometimes you have to call in the big guns. I like to call these people the covert ops of online reputation management. There are folks who can make things disappear from search results. It's a fairly exclusive thing and exactly how it works I can't explain, but we have worked with an organization that has been able to get stories and posts completely removed from search results using proprietary software.

These tactics are *not* the same thing as suppression, which pushes negative information further down the search results. I'm talking about either *removing* or *hiding* negative content.

Look at it this way. When you Google something, the information presented to you has passed through two sets of hands: the original source website and the search engine (Google) that found it and showed it to you. Therefore, to stop you from getting that information, the covert ops team has two places to attack: the original source website and the search engine. Engaging the source website—whether it's owned by the perpetrator or is a public platform like WordPress—may result in the information being removed. Engaging the search engine may result in the information being hidden from view. It's still there on the website, but only if someone knows exactly where to look.

Every website host and blogging platform has thousands of terms and conditions they must comply with to continue publishing. Many negative posts violate these terms and conditions, and they can either be removed from the site or hidden from Google search results. This approach isn't easy or inexpensive, but it can be done.

Search engine companies are incredibly sophisticated big businesses. As such, these organizations have thousands of standards and terms and conditions that they follow regarding publishing search results. There's such a vast amount of information published every day that they can't possibly check every single page and entry; this job is left to sophisticated algorithms. The covert ops companies, often run by former search company techies, know the vast terms and conditions and can work on your behalf to get negative information de-listed from sites like Google.

This means that the information still exists online, but it's hidden. It's no longer displayed by the search engines, which is all that really matters.

Each case is carefully processed using both proprietary software and human forensics. The source of the results is inspected, and this is then checked against the following:

the laws of the land

ISP terms of use

the hosting terms of use

the hosting site terms of use

Google terms and quality guidelines

motive and intent

background of the author

In fact, on any given search result, there can be more than 50 thousand points of regulation that can be assessed. The findings are then used to either hide the content from search engines or remove it from the source website.

Because these companies work behind the scenes, in most instances the original publisher of the negative information has no idea why the post disappeared from search engines. This area of reputation management is amazing and truly cutting edge, so you can imagine it comes at a heavy price tag. Be prepared to shell out tens of thousands of dollars for this service.

Case Study: Rick

One day a man whom I'll call Rick phoned me, and to say that he was in a panic is an understatement. He had a monster online problem and was not getting the answers he wanted from other online reputation management companies.

I was interested in hearing his story. Every online reputation problem is different, and I think it's impossible to properly assist a person with an online problem without first talking to them.

Rick had gone through a really bad breakup, and his ex-girlfriend had posted some incredibly nasty and incendiary comments about him on a blog site. Rick didn't do anything illegal or immoral but was perhaps not a perfect gentleman. His ex either knew exactly how to launch an online attack or came upon it by chance. Either way, Rick was freaking out.

Whether she knew what she was doing or fell into it, Rick's ex took a page right out of the online extremism playbook. She created an account on the blog site and then wrote a very detailed post that conclusively identified Rick. She posted his full name, his photograph, the city where he lived, and then details of why she found him to be disreputable. There was absolutely no doubt that the guy in the photo was Rick, and anyone who saw the photo would believe that the poster knew Rick. She didn't use language that would constitute hate speech, she didn't post any private information, and she did all of this in the context of warning other girls about Rick, which was a theme of the blog site. Then she deleted her account from the blog site and walked away—perhaps to watch from afar as her "online time bomb" exploded.

Rick is a wealthy executive, and he was deeply concerned about this post. When he called me, the nasty post was on page three of the Google search results for his name—and rising fast.

I gave him some options. First, we could reach out to the organization that hosted the blog and make an argument that the post was in violation of the site's terms and conditions. Second, we could engage in a suppression campaign to attempt to keep the item off the top pages of Google search. Third, he could discuss the situation with a lawyer specializing in defamation. Lastly, we could work with some consultants who specialize in tough cases. I call them the covert ops guys of online reputation management. Rick was interested in all options, and we started the first three immediately.

I reached out to the blog site directly and laid out a solid argument as to why I believed the post was in violation of their terms and conditions. The site where the incendiary remarks were made was something of a site within a site on the blogging platform, and it appeared to me that Rick's ex had registered for the internal site without having ever agreed to the main site's terms and conditions. While I thought it was a bit of clever analysis on my part, the owners of the website quickly responded by telling me to go take a hike.

We began a basic suppression campaign, which consisted of creating new digital assets based on Rick's name as the main search term. We secured his full name as a domain and built and optimized a vanity site for him. We also registered him on a number of social media sites and other destinations. This fortified his first page of search results, but after another week, the negative result stubbornly remained in the middle of page two of his search results.

We chose to build some additional digital assets, including a news release that officially announced a new consulting business. We distributed this using a private wire service, so the news release was published immediately on a number of high profile websites. Results from the news release took strong positions on pages one and two of search results, but we knew it would be a temporary fix.

We referred Rick to a defamation attorney who was sympathetic to his cause but said that unless he wanted to bring a full-blown defamation lawsuit against the woman, his options were minimal. Rick believed that legal action would only inflame his ex. It was also questionable whether his ex could afford to pay any damages. Even though there were legal options that may have been worth pursuing, none of them would solve Rick's problem in short order.

By the end of our second full week, the negative post was gaining steam and Rick was growing even more anxious.

Time for the big guns.

As part of my work in online reputation management, I've assembled a wide network of professionals to assist with different situations. I have web designers, social media specialists, publicists, and attorneys upon whom I can call for assistance. As I mentioned, one group specializes in tough cases, which I often refer to as the covert ops of reputation management.

The process works like this: Using propriety software, they analyze a website and review it against the thousands of terms and conditions with which every website must comply. In order for a site to be published online, it must comply with the terms of service required by the hosting company (such as GoDaddy and Network Solutions), the publishing platform (such as WordPress, Tumblr, or Blogger), search engines (like Google, Yahoo, or Bing) as well as major internet service providers (like AT&T, Verizon, and Comcast).

Thousands of terms and conditions exist across these platforms, and these specialists look for violations that could be leveraged to force the removal of the negative content at the hosting, website, or search engine level.

Essentially, they look for violations of terms of service and then engage the appropriate entity and make a case for removal of the negative information. While it's a complicated, technical, and sometimes time-consuming process, the results can be, by most reputation management standards, miraculous. The activities are completely above board, but even though I have worked with these online badasses on a number of projects, I'm not privy to the exact methodology.

Back to Rick. The covert ops team assessed Rick's situation, and we held a conference call to review the details. They determined that there were two links on Google search that were causing the most damage. One was on page two and the other on page three. The team told Rick that it could remove the negative links in a few weeks but it wouldn't come cheap. The cost was $11,000 per link, but only payable upon successful removal. Within 30 minutes of completing our teleconference, Rick signed the agreement.

For the next two weeks, we continued our suppression activities, consistently building and optimizing new assets for Rick. We kept control of page one for him as the covert ops guys worked their magic.

I spoke with Rick every day during this period, and he remained hopeful that the team would deliver. Then one day, the negative links were gone! Poof. Much to Rick's joy, they were completely gone from Google search results. The covert tactics worked as advertised.

Rick paid his bill and the search results never returned. In this case, the content had not simply been hidden; it had been removed. The covert ops experts had identified violations of terms and conditions that no other experts could find and then successfully convinced the website host to delete the negative content. When I tell people this story, most don't believe it, but I witnessed it and Rick paid for it.

It's Not a Perfect Science

So that's all there is to it? Just identify violations of terms and conditions and you can get anything you want taken down? Not so fast.

This specialized service does not work in all cases. Some hosting platforms are more amenable and responsive to violations of terms of service than others. Some blogging platforms take their rules more seriously than others. Certain search engines are more open to mediating and arbitrating abuse complaints than others. The success rate for removal of negative content is directly related to the above factors.

Some sites will *not* remove requests by these means. They include the following:

Government sites. Federal, state, and local websites are generally closed off to removal requests. For example, information about a stock broker losing his license on a regulatory agency's website or a news release published on a .gov website will be there forever.

High-profile news websites. Mainstream and top-tier news sites fall back on centuries of legal precedent to publish according to journalistic standards and will not remove articles and information from their sites. If a story was "true at the time of publication" and they can back it up with bona fide reporting, they won't change it or take it down. Stories on sites like NYTimes.com or Reuters.com will remain on those sites as long as the news agencies choose to keep them there.

Complaint sites. Online complaint sites, like RipoffReport.com, have long-standing policies, which they have defended by paying their expensive lawyers many thousands of dollars in legal fees, to never remove content from their sites. Other complaint sites follow the same model. While it may be possible to remove the link from search results with a court order, RipoffReport.com and other sites will not delete information.

Other Online Issues and How to Handle Them

A few years back, some enterprising folks decided to take advantage of people when they usually look their worst—in police booking photos or mugshots. ("Mug" is an English eighteenth-century slang term for "face.")

For decades, law enforcement agencies have been releasing mugshots. Without question, they are public documents that should be accessible by anyone. Until recently, they were most often published by bona fide news outlets like television stations and newspapers.

Such photo evidence serves a number of public purposes. Mugshots document the work done by law enforcement agencies and also create a visual catalog and record of prior offenders. Law enforcement agencies use the pictures for photo lineups, to keep track of criminals, and even for the FBI's Most Wanted list.

Sadly, some websites have also used publicly accessible mugshots to embarrass and extort individuals who have been arrested. Such individuals may be perfectly innocent of a crime, or they may have been subsequently convicted. Here's how it works.

The mugshot sites, of which there are dozens, pull mugshot images and related arrest information from public record searches and law enforcement databases. The sites then publish this information online and optimize the content for effective search engine results.

The mugshots frequently appear high on the search results for the arrested individual. Like complaint sites, mugshot sites benefit from having built large amounts of content over time, thus building their authority with the search engines. In recent years, Google has also made changes to its search algorithms and gives added influence to photographs and images.

The arrested person may then realize that people are seeing the mugshot listing when they are researching the individual for a job or another reason. The arrest record is often embarrassing and typically something that the individual doesn't want to broadcast.

Here's the moneymaking angle: The mugshot sites generally won't remove the listings unless you pay a fee. Sometimes, you are directed to another website that may "facilitate" the removal on your behalf, but also for a fee. In many cases, the mugshot site and the removal site are run by the same people. The bottom line is that if you don't pay the fee, the mugshot stays up on the site and therefore continues to be found on search results.

Does this sound like extortion? Some lawmakers think so. The mugshot sites claim that they are protected by free speech and that they are simply reproducing public records. This may be true, but many mugshot publishers also refuse to remove records for those who had their charges dropped, were expunged, or were found not guilty. Innocent individuals or those for whom the charges were dropped often appear to be guilty of a crime.

A few states have enacted laws that give mugshot sites 30 days to remove, for free, images of individuals who can show that charges were never filed or were dismissed, that the individual was acquitted or exonerated, or that the records were expunged. In addition, a number of jails and municipalities have implemented policies to no longer publish mugshots, making it harder for the booking photos sites to operate.

I spoke to a criminal defense attorney who was pleased that many police departments were no longer releasing mugshots but explained that unfortunately the best option for many individuals is to pay the removal fee, which is typically around $400. To hire an attorney to fight it would likely cost more than to pay what adds up to be an extortion fee.

Expunged Records May Be Removed from Search Results

Much to the chagrin of folks who are trying to put their past misdeeds behind them, some criminal records are easily found on-line on public or government websites. In some cases, criminal records can be hidden from the public. As I have said previously, I'm not an attorney so I can't give legal advice, but my understanding is that expungement might be an option for some folks who have had criminal issues. Expungement is a court-ordered process that results in an arrest or criminal conviction being sealed. Such records are not erased, as they remain accessible by law enforcement and government agencies, but they generally will not show up on background checks. It's as if you had never been arrested. In some states, you also can legally deny that you committed an offense or were arrested.

Laws regarding expungement vary from state to state, and some legal matters may not be eligible for it. If you have an arrest record that you would like expunged, my recommendation is that you contact an attorney for proper legal counsel.

Whether or not a private website will comply with a removal request of an expunged arrest record is open to interpretation. Some sites may remove a negative post backed up by an expunged record, so it is likely worth the effort to try. News outlets are unlikely to comply, as they will say that information that was true at the time of publication will not be removed from their site.

Cyberbullying and Cyberstalking

Often used interchangeably by the media, cyberbullying and cyberstalking are terms that typically refer to situations where someone uses the internet or other electronic means to stalk or harass an individual, group, or organization. Cyberstalking is considered a form of cyberbullying. It may also include threats, vandalism, identity theft, monitoring, and real time, in-person stalking. Regardless if it is online or offline, stalking is considered a form of mental assault and is illegal. Cyberbullying, more frequently associated with children and teens, is bullying that takes place using electronic technology such as cell phones and computers as well as social media sites, text messages, and websites. In my opinion, anyone who believes they or their loved ones are a victim of cyberbullying or cyberstalking should contact the police immediately.

Google Will Remove Certain Content Used in Online Attacks

While the internet may still be viewed by some as the Wild West, Google and the other major search engines have made efforts to remove some online content that has little redeeming value or can cause significant damage. In 2015, for example, Google announced it would enable victims of revenge porn to ask that the search company remove from its search engine links to websites that post intimate photos or videos posted online without the subject's consent.

"Our philosophy has always been that search should reflect the whole Web," Amit Singhal, senior vice president of Google Search, said in a blog post at the time. "But revenge porn images are intensely personal and emotionally damaging, and serve only to degrade the victim—predominantly women."

Microsoft, the owner of Bing, quickly followed suit.

Google says it will remove revenge porn search results in the same way it does other sorts of highly sensitive personal information such as bank account numbers and Social Security numbers. At the time of this writing, Google has created and implemented policies to remove the following types of items, among others, from search results:

child sexual abuse imagery

content targeted by a valid legal request, such as copyright notifications that meet the requirements of the Digital Millennium Copyright Act

national identification numbers like a U.S. Social Security number

bank account numbers

credit card numbers

images of signatures

an inappropriate, malicious, or spammy site

a pornographic site that contains a full name or business name

According to Google, to determine if a piece of information creates significant risk of identity theft, financial fraud, or other specific harm, it asks the following questions:

Is it a government-issued identification number?

Is it confidential, or is it publicly available information?

Can it be used for common financial transactions?

Can it be used to obtain more information about an individual that would result in financial harm or identity theft?

Is it a personally identifiable nude or sexually explicit photo or video shared without consent?

Google says it applies this policy on a case-by-case basis. If it believes that a removal request is being used to attempt to remove unrelated, non-personal information from search results, it will deny the request. It's important to note that Google typically asks that anyone requesting to have content removed from its search engine should first contact the webmaster of the site in question.

Google does process many removal requests, though. It often receives more than 10 million removal requests per week for copyright infringement cases for such things as pirated music and copyright protected photos and videos.

In 2014, Google unveiled a system that enables citizens of the European Union to ask the search engine to remove results from its listings. The move comes in response to a landmark E.U. court ruling that gave people there the "right to be forgotten."

Europeans who want personal information removed from search results can make their case directly to Google via an online form. And even though, as with everything with Google, the requests must be made online, the final decision on what information will be removed from search results will be made by actual people, not one of Google's famed algorithms. According a story from the BBC, disagreements about whether information should be removed or not will be overseen by national data protection agencies.

While this news was biggest in Europe, it also affected the ongoing debate in the United States about privacy and information posted on the internet about private U.S. citizens. It makes me wonder what qualifies as something falling under the right to be forgotten and if such a policy might find its way to U.S. shores.

For starters, this new policy is only going into effect for countries within the European Union. Google's submission form asks what country you're from, and the United States is not an option. Further, Google requires that anyone asking for personal information to be removed provide identification, so you can't make a removal request on behalf of someone else.

But who and what deserves to be forgotten? This is a fascinating debate that might rage for a long time. The BBC article included a sidebar about a man in England who lost his job after his employer learned of a drunk driving conviction that preceded his employment. The man was never asked about it on his employment application, but after he had been hired, someone found evidence of his conviction online, and he was sacked. This man believed he had the right to have his drunk driving conviction forgotten. (It's important to note that while the story didn't describe the man's vocation, it did say that he was not a chauffeur, bus driver, or the like.) He had made a mistake that he hoped would not continue to haunt him.

To me, this seems like a reasonable request that Google could grant. Yet the waters are so much murkier. Having grown up before the digital age, I'm fortunate that the things I hope remain forgotten (#fraternity, #college) were never cataloged online. Folks who have had indiscretions since the rise of the internet are not as lucky. Does a person have the right to have a photo of them taking a bong hit removed from search? Perhaps so. But what if that person were a public figure like Olympic swimmer Michael Phelps? Maybe not. If Kim Kardashian decided to ditch her camera-obsessed ways and live a monastic lifestyle in Montana, would she deserve to someday be forgotten? We'd probably say no, because she's a public figure and famous.

But what about infamy? Would we no longer have a right to exploit that? Does Chicago Cubs fan Steve Bartman have a right to have his infamous foul-ball-interference moment forgotten? While Cubs fans will never forget how he may have cheated them of a World Series appearance, does he have a right to be removed from search results?

While the right to have some personal information removed from web searches is currently confined to the European Union, it seems that this right has potential to migrate across the Atlantic. I have a friend who was born in Wales but married an American. He holds dual citizenship, so could he ask for information to be removed from search using his British passport as identification but submitting it from his office in Florida? Can I finally cash in on my Polish ancestry and make an argument that I'm as European as my long-lost relatives on that continent?

And here's another question: What if Google's efforts in the European Union turn out to be well received and uncontroversial? Might the worldwide search engine itself migrate the policies to the United States and the rest of the planet?

I will leave the legal arguments to the attorneys and free-speech advocates, but it seems to me that, while tricky to judge, the right to be forgotten is an intriguing option that could find its way to America. I wouldn't expect to see it anytime soon, but it's certainly worthy of discussion.

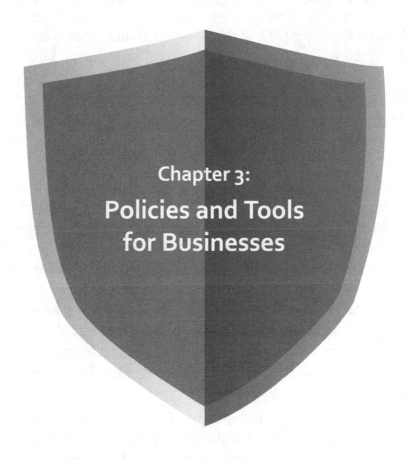

Chapter 3:

Policies and Tools for Businesses

Online reputation risks are often multiplied for businesses, as companies need to look far beyond how search results impact one person's name. Businesses need to protect their company names, their brands, and their products from many online threats. Negative online reviews can hurt sales, social media missteps can open up a company to costly litigation, and reputational risks may even lurk beneath the surface of the web.

Online and offline reputation are quickly merging. Today, traditional word-of-mouth advertising is amplified by online channels, and customer service often begins with an online interaction through a public social media channel.

Whether companies like it or not, customers have learned that reaching out to companies on sites like Twitter often elicits a response more quickly than calling a customer service line. If an employee's connection to a company is known on social media, then it is very possible that he may be contacted by a customer. And in some instances, customers specifically try to go around customer service departments to get questions answered—or if they are frustrated.

Last year, my wife, Pamela, was shopping for a new health insurance plan for our family. Aetna had made some changes and announced it was discontinuing our plan, which caused confusion for us as a deadline to select a new plan was looming. Pamela called Aetna customer service, concerned that we might be without health coverage in the coming weeks. She spent much of an afternoon on hold with Aetna, as the company was seemingly overwhelmed with calls. I'm not talking about 10–15 minute hold times either. She was on hold for nearly two hours and didn't get a resolution. Frustrated and angry, she gave up, convinced that there must have been a technical problem at the call center.

The next morning, she called me and said she was again stuck on an unconscionable hold with Aetna and asked if I would reach out to the company on Twitter. I did a quick search, found a top executive from Aetna, and sent a tweet, bemoaning the hold times and asking for help. Within a few minutes, an Aetna representative reached out to me and asked if I could send a Twitter direct message that explained the issue.

I did just that, and later that day, Pamela was able to have a productive conversation with a customer service representative from Aetna, and our issue was finally resolved. Had we not reached out via Twitter, she might still be on hold.

Today, many consumers, and millennials in particular, have an expectation that a company will respond on social media channels. This is bolstered by the fact that many major corporations are effectively using Twitter as a customer service channel. Companies like Zappos, Nike, and UPS actively engage customers on Twitter, which promotes this use of its platform and offers specific tools for businesses. For instance, a business can now easily add a link to their tweets that automatically displays a call to action button, which allows the customer to send the business a Twitter direct message. Some businesses are receiving a growing number of customer service requests through social media, and they are embracing it because in some cases, it is significantly cheaper than staffing a call center. In fact, many businesses now include their Twitter handles on their customer service pages, giving customers an option to either call, e-mail, or reach out on Twitter.

The ability to contact a company via social media has changed the dynamics of customer service, and new responsibility lands in the hands of all employees of the organization. First, employees should know that customers my contact them via social media with questions and complaints. They should be prepared, through an understanding of the company's formal social media policy, to respond appropriately and direct the request to the correct person within the organization.

Second, employees should, in general, keep an eye out for social media mentions of the company. Several companies that I researched included sections in their social media policies where they ask employees to act as "scouts" for the organization. Corporations have realized that employees, even if they are not spokespeople or working in a communications department, are valuable assets in monitoring the social media landscape. The policies suggest that employees who come across remarks about the company, positive or negative, should share them with the communications department of the organization as soon as possible.

One drug company even makes specific mention of social media posts that discuss side effects of taking the company's drugs. Employees who come across such posts are instructed to immediately forward such information to the company's global drug safety team.

Social media has entered the corporate culture of many businesses, particularly as it relates to customer service. The Hotel Commonwealth in Boston has abandoned customer comment cards and instead tells its employees to direct its guests to TripAdvisor to leave feedback about their stay. The online travel review site has become a critical component of its customer service strategy and its primary means to receive direct feedback.

Other companies include social media and review sites in their overall customer service strategy. Simply adding a link to Yelp on the auto signature of customer service representatives can increase exposure on that site—and in a way that won't go astray from that site's nitpicky policies.

In general, employees need to be aware that their business and online lives may intersect, whether they like it or not, and that they need to act accordingly if it happens.

Social Media Monitoring Keeps Your Eye on the Web

The concept of social media monitoring runs the gamut from free methods and tools, which can be used by anyone, to sophisticated software that digs deeper than a typical Google search and enables a user to see beyond paywalls—but for a price that may be outside the realm for most businesses. Regardless of where your business falls in the spectrum, social media monitoring should be part of your marketing mix.

Why monitor? More than 400 years ago, Sir Francis Bacon said "knowledge is power." Monitoring social media channels enables a business to track online reputation issues as they happen, if need be. Such knowledge can help avert a crisis. While many of us will probably be okay with checking our social media feeds daily or even less frequently, some organizations are better served with real-time monitoring—or at least a systemized approach that alerts them of potential online brush fires.

Monitoring represents the first step toward online engagement and proves useful for both customer service and reputation management. Knowing what people are saying as soon as possible offers the most options for engagement and response.

Free tools abound. Many individuals and businesses are keenly aware of free tools for monitoring online activity. Google alerts can be quickly and easily configured to send a user an e-mail when they or their company is mentioned on Google. This can be set up to cover the entire web so that an alert is sent as soon as it is detected by Google. Or alerts can be sent daily or weekly and only focus on news outlets or other specific types of information such as blogs, video, books, etc. Google alerts can focus on a particular region or all of Earth, and they can also be configured to only send the most relevant results.

Twitter accounts can be configured to send the user notifications when they are mentioned on the site, and Facebook will also notify you when someone comments on your page. Nearly every social media site can enable notifications by e-mail, and most offer such services for free.

Third-party services like TweetDeck and Hootsuite enable users to monitor numerous social media feeds through an online dashboard. Costs range from free for basic versions to monthly subscriptions based on the number of users and whether or not you want access to additional tools and analytics.

Monitoring gets more complicated if you want to track multiple locations, brands, keywords, or people. It's easy to end up with multiple Google alerts pinging your phone at all hours of the day and a wide variety of e-mails hitting your inbox notifying you of comments and mentions on social media sites. It can quickly become overwhelming, particularly for large enterprises.

Information technology firms offer a solution for monitoring that can make the entire process better organized and offer sophisticated analysis along with other interesting features—but at a price. For example, some online monitoring services will continuously track your online reputation on news sites, blogs, and social media sites and can be programmed to send a comprehensive report, say every business morning, that lists all of your company's mentions from the previous 24 hours—along with the same information for your competitors. In addition, a monitoring algorithm will analyze the articles, blog posts, tweets, and Facebook comments for tone, typically scoring mentions as positive, negative, or neutral.

Such systems can then compare and contrast your organization's online activity with that of your competitors and determine if one entity has a greater share of social media or traditional media activity. So-called share of voice reports can help judge the effectiveness of your marketing efforts against those of your competitors.

Monitoring services can also create reports of media and online activity as it relates to your entire industry, helping a company's executives stay abreast of the latest industry news. In fact, some services work in conjunction with existing media databases so that news articles can be viewed and read even if they are behind paywalls or are posted on sites that require a subscription. This by itself can be valuable as many Google searches can pull up news articles that can't be viewed in their entirety without a subscription.

Comprehensive online monitoring can be an incredibly effective tool. Imagine receiving a daily report that highlights the traditional media and online media exposure of your company as well as that of your competitors and also analyzes it for share of voice. In addition, all members of your executive team can receive the report via e-mail with clickable links that enable all team members to read relevant news articles—even if they are behind a paywall. It's a powerful tool.

Software systems like this also enable users to perform comprehensive searches on an as needed basis. So a new product launch can be accurately tracked or the daily report can be modified to include new keywords, competitors, or industry terms. Subscriptions to monitoring services like the one I describe can easily top $10,000 per year, and prices go higher depending on the number of users and how comprehensive the searches become. Yet, if viewed as a cost of doing business within today's social media landscape and contrasted against the cost to remedy an online misstep, such a cost could be easily justified.

Develop Critical Social Media Policies

Many highly publicized social media slipups involve individuals posting information online that ends up costing them their jobs. Sadly, such situations are numerous. In fact, a 2015 CareerBuilder survey found that 18 percent of companies have fired an employee for something posted on social media.[1] Posting disrespectful or offensive statements, publishing photos or videos of illegal or reckless behavior, and posting rants about an employer or co-worker are typical problems. In other situations, employees post private or confidential information online or improperly or accidentally post information that can be construed as an official opinion of the company. Such situations can be mitigated and sometimes prevented if companies establish and adhere to a social media policy.

In 2012, Adam Smith was the chief financial officer of an Arizona medical device company and earning more than $200,000 per year.[2] Upset with restaurant chain Chick-fil-A's support of organizations that are hostile to LGBT causes, Smith visited a restaurant in his area and recorded his interaction with an employee working at the drive-through window. Smith, with the video recording, proceeded to berate the employee and say that it was shameful that she was working for Chick-fil-A, calling it a "hateful" company among other insults.

Smith then posted the video to YouTube, but it didn't have the desired effect. Instead of fueling the anger of other anti-Chick-fil-A activists, the video went viral due to Smith's bullying of the restaurant worker. To her credit, the employee took the high road, smiled, and treated Smith with much more respect than he afforded her.

Major news organizations published stories about Smith's bullying and liberally played the clip. One commentator said "if you have a grudge against the CEO of a major corporation, only an idiot would go on a rampage against a front-line staffer."

Smith's employer fired him shortly thereafter and the video (and his behavior) have prevented him from securing new employment. In 2015, it was reported by multiple news sources that Smith remained unemployed, and he and his family were collecting food stamps.

In 2011, an employee of a Chrysler public relations firm posted this tweet on a then-official Twitter page: "I find it ironic that Detroit is known as the Motorcity and yet no one here knows how to f***ing drive."[3] The employee responsible for the tweet was fired and the public relations agency lost the contract.

In 2009, the Facebook page for Honda's new Crosstour was overflowing with negative comments about the design and look of the vehicle. (Sadly, it is not the prettiest car.) Honda employee Eddie Okubo chose to post how much he liked the design but failed to disclose that he worked for the car company.[4] The internet struck back as Facebook users quickly identified Okubo as a shill, dealing an embarrassing online blow to Honda. The company later removed the post, noting that Okubo failed to identify himself as a Honda employee who was offering his personal opinion and because he was not an official spokesperson for the brand.

In many of these instances, the big loser is the employee. We don't get upset with the company that fired Smith for his bullying video. We don't blame Chrysler for ditching the public relations firm that made the egregious error. And we don't blame Honda for Okubo's comment as it appeared that he was acting alone—though I imagine some folks may believe otherwise.

In some situations though, confidential information is distributed online with varying consequences—causing reputational, financial, and legal damage to businesses. In 2012, publicly traded fashion retailer Francesca's Holdings Corp. fired CFO Gene Morphis, citing that he "improperly communicated company information through social media." Morphis had a history of tweeting non-public information about the company, but one instance was particularly significant. The *Wall Street Journal* reported that six words likely caused Morphis his job when he tweeted "Board meeting. Good numbers=Happy Board." At the time, Francesca's was in a quiet period prior to the release of earnings a week later. The information derived from the tweet, then non-public, helped send the company stock price surging 15 percent during the week before the earnings were released.[5] Morphis's giddy tweet exposed Francesca's to scrutiny from the Securities and Exchange Commission and potentially individual or corporate penalties that range from $50,000 to $500,000, according to analysis by securities attorneys.

In 2012, Netflix CEO Reed Hastings made the following post on his personal Facebook page: "Congrats to Ted Sarandos, and his amazing content licensing team. Netflix monthly viewing exceeded 1 billion hours for the first time ever in June. When House of Cards and Arrested Development debut, we'll blow these records away. Keep going, Ted, we need even more!"[6]

The offering of kudos by Hastings allegedly violated rules governing selective disclosure. The post appeared on the same day that shares in the company rose 6.2 percent, marking its share price's largest gain in six weeks. Netflix and Hastings were each issued Wells Notices, letters that the SEC sends to people or firms when it is planning to bring an enforcement action against them.

In 2014, Twitter Chief Financial Officer Anthony Noto publicly tweeted a message that was likely meant to be a private direct message: "I still think we should buy them. He is on your schedule for Dec 15 or 16--we will need to sell him. i have a plan."[7] The tweet was quickly deleted but fueled speculation in the investment community that publicly traded Twitter Inc. was attempting to acquire the comedy app Shots. The acquisition never happened, and it is unclear if the tweet had an impact on that decision. Regardless, in the high stakes world of Wall Street mergers and acquisitions, it's never a good idea to tell the public what your plans are. (Noto remained the Twitter CFO.)

In these instances, the social media posts of top executives, not ill-informed part-time or low-level workers, exposed publicly traded companies to potential fines and legal fees that could total hundreds of thousands of dollars. Even though the SEC announced new disclosure rules in 2013 that clarified how corporations can use social media sites to distribute information, it remains abundantly clear that companies, both large and small, need to have social media policies in place to prevent long-term damage.

A social media policy should include the following components:

Remind employees that offline rules apply to online activities. Most companies have an employment agreement or handbook that offers guidance on employee conduct. A social media policy should include a reminder that the guidelines in the employee handbook apply not only to traditional offline activities but online conduct as well. For example, public companies like Coca-Cola explain in their social media policies that every employee, from interns to the chairman of the board, must adhere to the company's standards of conduct in every public setting. This includes business conduct, confidentiality, and rules against insider trading. And the social policy media reminds employees that these rules apply to personal online activities.

Define social media. A social media policy should clearly state what types of communications are included in the guidelines. Companies should expect employees to follow the guidelines in nearly all online public means of communicating. Some organizations refer to this as "web participation" and define it as all forms of public web-based communication and expression, including blogs, microblogs, social network sites, wikis, bookmark sites, content sharing sites, forums, mailing lists, discussion groups, and chat rooms.

Reinforce commitment to confidentiality. Companies and their clients have an expectation of confidentiality, and this should be reinforced in social media policies. For example, employees should not discuss financial information, sales trends, business strategies, company forecasts, legal issues, or future promotional activities. In addition, employees at all levels should not post information or advice that clients otherwise pay for. One consulting firm says it plainly in its policy: Don't "give away the farm." And as we learned from the example with Francesca's and Mr. Morphis, employees should never disclose non-public information.

Promote disclosure. Disclosure represents a critical yet confusing aspect of a social media policy as guidance may differ from company to company and even from employee to employee. For example, an employee of a chain retail store may not be required to disclose their professional affiliation on social media sites like Facebook or Twitter. Yet, if that same employee chooses to comment on something regarding their employer in a public forum, then they should disclose their employment when making a comment. A good rule of thumb is that an employee should be the first to identify their employer—and not wait to be asked during an interaction on social media.

In some cases, individuals should publicly identify themselves on social media accounts no matter what. For example, if you are an analyst for a technology firm, and you post on your personal page about technology issues, you may open yourself up to risk if you don't disclose the name of your employer. The same can be true of C-level executives and officers of publicly traded companies. Any statements made on social media can be misconstrued, so it is best to disclose who you work for.

In other instances, employers may prohibit employees from participating in specific online discussions. One technology company specifically states in its social media policy that employees may not initiate or maintain a personal blog, discussion group, or site that discusses the company, its business, or the entire information technology industry.

While it may seem that discussing business on social media accounts is completely fraught with peril, many companies encourage their employees to participate on social media, and some mainstream media outlets require it of their reporters and producers. Here it is even more critical to offer details on how to behave.

Some companies want you to be on social media and be visible—such as media outlets—but you have to be careful that you don't endorse a particular point of view. For example, members of the media should be certain that social media posts are properly attributed. A simple re-tweet could be deemed as passing editorial judgment in favor or against another online item. In fact, some national media outlets disagree on whether a re-tweet constitutes an endorsement. National Public Radio says yes. The *New York Times* says no.

Offer disclaimers. While a disclaimer on a social media profile does not absolve the author from responsibility, it is a good practice to post that opinions expressed on the site are yours and not those of your employer. For example, some executives include wording like this on their profiles: "The views expressed are mine alone and do not necessarily reflect the views of [your employer]."

Don't make it look official. Employees may be proud that they work for a company or organization, but including a logo on a social media profile suggests that it is an official page.

Respect copyright, privacy, fair use, and other laws. All employees should be aware of copyright, privacy, and fair use laws, particularly when publishing on behalf of a company. Words written by or images created by another person are protected by copyright laws. In some instances, images and excerpts can be used, but it is always best to get permission from the source and discuss the issue with the employer's marketing or legal department.

Of course, many social media sites are littered with images that infringe on copyright laws. I'm sure that many individuals have inadvertently posted copyrighted material. In fact, I have had large sections of my personal blog posts copied nearly word for word by other bloggers. While such activity is in violation of my copyright, I have never sued anyone for it—but I have asked them to either take it down or at least give me appropriate credit for my ideas and writings. Things get sticky when a company violates copyright laws as it can open a business up to costly litigation.

Don't act as a spokesperson. In some cases, employees may feel the need to respond to statements made online about their employers or the products they sell. My best advice is that they don't. A social media policy should direct the employee to an official spokesperson for the company, typically someone in communications, marketing, or public relations. Company experts are best equipped to deal with negative comments or address specific concerns.

Make sure you have permission to post on company pages. Just as a company spokesperson should address comments and concerns on social media sites, only approved employees should be posting information to a company social media page.

Employers reserve the right to avoid subjects and may ask you to take stuff down. All companies respect an employee's right to free speech, and few have time to monitor all of the online interactions of their workers. However, some companies may ask that employees steer clear of particular subjects that may be controversial or inflammatory. Employees should be aware that it may be within their employer's rights to ask an employee to take a post down. Bad behavior could be a violation of an employment agreement or could lead to quick termination, particularly for at-will employees.

Know when to get help. With social media participation comes mistakes. Without them, I wouldn't have written this book. A social media policy should give clear guidance on what an employee should do if they make a mistake. Typically, correcting the error does the trick, but for big errors, employees should quickly contact their supervisor, a senior executive, social media manager, or public relations staff person.

Use common sense and good judgment. The easiest way to stay out of trouble online is to exercise common sense and good judgment. Employees need to understand that they are responsible for their actions and anything they post has the potential to tarnish the image of their employer. Employers recommend that workers think before they post and think about the reactions others may have— before information is posted. Have respect for the audience on social media and avoid negative personal comments or inflammatory subjects. Note that customers, co-workers, and supervisors may see the content that is posted. Publishing information can often be forwarded or copied and then seen by more than just friends and family. Remind employees that their jobs come first and not to let use of social media impact job performance.

Sample Social Media Policy

Below is a sample social media policy. Note that a document such as this may be incorporated into an employee handbook, and my recommendation is that it be reviewed by your company's legal counsel prior to distribution to employees.

Social Media Policy for Our Company

1. Our company's corporate policies and those found in the employee handbook apply to both offline and online behavior. All employees must follow the guidelines.

2. At our company, we define social media usage and web participation as all forms of public web-based

communication and expression, including blogs, microblogs, social network sites, wikis, bookmark sites, content sharing sites, forums, mailing lists, discussion groups, and chat rooms.

3. While we encourage use of social media by our employees, we ask that you use sound judgment. Have respect for the audience on social media and avoid negative personal comments or inflammatory subjects. Note that customers, co-workers, and supervisors may see the content that is posted. Also, personal social media usage should not interfere with your core job responsibilities.

4. While we ask that only our official spokespeople comment publicly on behalf of the company, we do know that your employment with our company may be known among others on social media. Always be the first to disclose your affiliation with our company, if possible well before a situation becomes controversial.

5. All employees of our company have access to how we do business, while some are entrusted with confidential information. Remember to keep the company's private information private and our confidential information confidential.

6. Remember that we have designated spokespeople to deal with direct inquiries. Avoid the temptation to respond on behalf of our company, and forward any inquiries to your supervisor or a designated spokesperson.

7. While you may be proud of your affiliation with our company, please refrain from including our company logo on your social media profiles.

8. At our company, we respect your rights of expression and encourage your participation in organizations and causes. Please consider a disclaimer on social media

profiles such as "views expressed are mine alone," particularly when addressing controversial topics.

9. Know that we are here to help with social media questions. Contact your supervisor or the communications department with any issues. All questions are good questions.

10. Have fun on social media and try to keep an eye out for our company if you can. We would love your help in identifying situations where we have done well or fallen short with our customers.

Responding to Social Media Feedback

When monitoring social media for customer feedback, follow a few simple procedures for customers who post comments on Facebook or make statements on Twitter or use other social media networks to contact a company.

Document feedback. A procedure should be established to make a copy of the complaint via a screen capture or other method so that it can be documented for future reference. Perhaps create a folder for each day, week, or month depending on the volume of online feedback, and each complaint should be individually dated as well.

Act quickly. Most online feedback is not life or death, and most customers have reasonable expectations about how long it will take to receive a response. Many companies suggest that online comments must receive a response within one business day. Some larger companies give responses within hours, as they choose to use social media as a main channel for customer service inquiries. Most consumers can wait a day without needing to escalate.

Respond publicly but work to move the conversation offline. Customers who reach out via social media channels have an expectation that they will receive a response through the same channel. Companies should respond via the social media site but then work to move the conversation offline. First, neither customers nor a business should want to handle such matters in public. Second, legal and privacy concerns may come into play. A response via social media should always offer a way for the company and customer to connect offline by phone, by e-mail, or even by private direct message.

Don't delete negative comments. While it may seem like an easy solution to delete negative comments, this is a slippery slope. We live in an age when customers are demanding transparency and simply deleting negative feedback will come back to haunt your company as your integrity will be questioned. Feedback that is profane, hateful, or defamatory should be removed as should spam or sales pitches masked as comments.

Ensure a tone of professionalism. If you think about it, an online interaction may turn out to be the first and only time a customer actually engages with a company, so this interaction should be professional in tone. Employees who are entrusted with the job of responding to customers online should be trained to be customer-focused and strive to offer exceptional service. Like the old saying, you only get one chance to make a first impression.

Sort and redirect. Odds are that the employee who is in charge of reviewing social media feedback will not have the knowledge and experience to handle the details and nuances of every complaint. A procedure should be in place to sort and redirect online feedback to an appropriate division, department, or individual.

Take ownership and follow through. Customer frustration can be appeased by interaction, but it only gets worse if the customer feels like they are getting lip service. Individuals who interact with customers online should have involvement with the entire customer service process or have a clear line when ownership of a customer interaction changes hands. Customers don't expect that the person who replied to them on social media will ultimately solve their problem, but they certainly will not want to go back to that person if someone else drops the ball.

Media Relations Policy: An Important Asset During a Crisis

If you are dealing with a communications situation of any kind, but particularly a crisis, it is important that an organization speak with one voice, meaning that any official communications from the organization should come from a designated spokesperson. A clear media relations policy can be invaluable as it serves as a reminder to employees that only authorized spokespeople should communicate with members of the press, and it also offers guidance on how to handle media inquiries.

We want employees to be courteous to members of the press but state very clearly that they are not authorized to speak on behalf of the company. Employees should then direct media inquiries to a spokesperson, a member of the communications team, or even a company's public relations firm.

Below is a sample corporate media policy. A document similar to this is often part of an employee handbook and may require review or approval by your legal team. I believe that employees should regularly be reminded of your company's media policy, and a document similar to the one below should be circulated to employees if your company is facing media scrutiny or if a media crisis is impending.

Media Relations Policy for Our Company

Our company maintains an open working relationship with the media. We are committed to working with the media in order to maximize our visibility through coverage and enhance our reputation as a good corporate citizen. We encourage media coverage and opportunities for positive exposure through the press, and we have to generate and make the most of media coverage for our company.

<u>Policies and Practices</u>

In all of our dealings with the media, it is critical for our company to maintain consistent messages and deliver the most pertinent and effective information to interested journalists. Therefore, we have instituted the following media policy, which must be adhered to by all employees in order for us to manage and capitalize on all of the media opportunities that become available:

1. Only our company's CEO John Smith is authorized to speak to members of the press as a spokesperson for our company. [You can designate more than one person, if need be.]

   • Mr. Smith can be reached at [enter e-mail] or [enter phone number].

2. All media communications, including telephone calls, meetings, news releases, letters, e-mails, story suggestions, and industry commentary, will be developed and distributed by our company's authorized spokespeople or under their supervision and direction. Employees who have a media communications suggestion are encouraged to share it with them for consideration.

3. If any employee is contacted by a member of the press regarding any issue related to our company or our industry in general, they must respond with the utmost courtesy and convey to the journalist that, because they are not an authorized spokesperson for our company, they will not be able to respond and instead must refer their questions to Mr. Smith. Ask for the journalist's telephone number, media affiliation, and deadline status and convey this information along as soon as conveniently possible with any specific questions.

4. If Mr. Smith is not available, relay the inquiry and contact information to our company's public relations firm, David PR Group. The firm can be reached at [enter phone number].

- Its principal John P. David can be reached at [enter e-mail] or [enter mobile phone number].

Online Feedback: The Blessing and Curse of Businesses

For years, the public relations sales pitch included a reminder that "perception is reality." Whether we like it or not, how we are viewed by others helps define us. But the definition of perception is actually changing, and it's not just the mental image that people have of us that matters. Today, we have to look beyond traditional mental imagery and also focus on how we're perceived digitally. Perception is also digital reality.

Through web searches, review sites, and social media channels, the internet has become the front door for most businesses. In most cases, the first impression and the initial perception that people will have about you and your company will come through the web.

Searches on Google, Facebook, and LinkedIn, along with reviews from sites like TripAdvisor and Yelp, dramatically influence how we are perceived. If we fail to take control of our digital front door, then we're inviting disruptive forces to our branding party.

Online reviews are not going away, and I mean that in both the literal and figurative senses. It is difficult to get negative reviews removed, especially from large review sites, and some websites have made a business of posting negative information about companies and individuals. Because they won't just go away on their own, negative reviews have to be countered. Further, time has shown that consumers like to look at reviews and read feedback on businesses that they may patronize.

While some businesses (retail, restaurants, hotels) feel the most impact from reviews, Google offers the ability to review any business that has a Google Places listing. Doctors, hospitals, and healthcare providers have increasingly been feeling the impact.

The fewer reviews a business has, the more vulnerable it is to having one negative review torpedo its overall ranking. Tools exist to make gaining positive reviews more systematic, so it pays to investigate them.

At one company, a customer was so upset that they posted negative reviews on several review sites and complaint sites. The customer even created a hate page on Facebook. The online attacks were so effective that the negative content dominated the first two pages of search results. I reviewed the situation, which included taking a closer look at the negative Facebook page. A few weeks later, while browsing my personal Facebook feed, I was surprised to see that the creators of the hate page were promoting it. I was being asked, through a promoted offering that the haters had to pay for, if I wanted to join and like the hate page of the company! As I mentioned, if someone is mad, mean, and clever enough, they can do tremendous damage to a company and its brand.

In another instance, a large company with multiple offices and hundreds of corporate clients completely neglected review sites for years, and eventually the problem escalated to the point that a solution became very difficult. Though I don't like to hold myself out as a search engine optimization expert, there are several well-known factors that influence search results. One is the age of a page. In this example, the fact that the only reviews available on this company were negative and had been on sites like

Yelp and Yellow Pages for years gave these reviews high authority with search engines—authority that was higher than had they only been a few months old. One colleague suggested that the only viable online reputation solution for this decades-old company was to change its name.

Name a major brand and it probably has a hate site: Apple, McDonald's, Coca-Cola, Chevy, and so on. The sites are easy to find, but they don't appear high in search results when you're looking for general information on the brands. Companies like Apple, for example, have so much positive information on the web, and loyal customers who author positive reviews, that the good news largely drowns out the bad.

Small businesses aren't as fortunate. If you run a local business, a few negative reviews can be killers, particularly if you have been late to the online review party. A whole generation of able-bodied spenders known as the millennials have grown up with the internet, and they are very likely to check out your online reputation prior to purchasing, even if your products aren't offered directly for sale online. Businesses that ignore the internet and the power of reviews do so at their peril.

The Business of Complaint Sites

Sometimes I wonder if complaining is our national pastime. Traffic, our in-laws, and customer service are typical targets.

Complaining is also big business, particularly online. Just a few years ago, as in before the internet, we only had a few ways to complain about products, retailers, or customer service. We could call a company's customer service department, ask to speak to the manager at a store, or, if we were really upset, write a letter (yeah, on paper) to the president of a company.

Today, making a complaint can be done in a matter of clicks, and we can do it even before we leave a retail establishment, restaurant, or hotel. We can contact a company directly through its website or via e-mail, send a tweet to that same company's president, or post a complaint on a consumer complaint website.

Don't get me wrong; I'm all for good customer service and accountability in business. The ability to communicate more directly with companies about their products and services certainly keeps businesses on their toes. However, it has also made consumer complaint websites very powerful, opening the door for misinformation, competitor bashing, and unreasonable complaints.

Sites such as RipoffReport.com, Complaints.com, ComplaintsBoard .com, Scam.com, and TheDirty.com have learned that complaints and negative posts can track high on search results. The concept is a game changer that turns complaints into money-making machines:

- Users create content for a site by posting complaints.
- The bigger the site grows, the greater its authority with search engines.
- More visitors from searches means more complaints, more ad revenues, and so on and so on.

These sites are not just about consumer protection; in fact, many of them only mildly address such values. The sites are generally open forums that enable anyone to say whatever they want, without any policing or commitment to accuracy. The First Amendment and the laws of the digital land protect them from defamation lawsuits.

Many of these sites go to great lengths to explain why they are protected from legal claims regarding content posted on their sites. Scam.com, for example, lists the legal cases that back their position of allowing anyone to post without care for accuracy.

ComplaintsBoard.com explains that it is not responsible for verifying the validity of consumer complaints, providing responses, or notifying those on the receiving end of complaints. It also says that it will only remove a posted complaint if ordered to by a court. And here's a great little nugget of effrontery: The complaint site says that it assumes that the writers of complaints have positive intents.

PissedConsumer.com and TheDirty.com are proponents of this scorched-earth policy. On one hand, it's freedom of speech at its best. On the other, it's opening the door for anyone to say whatever they want, without any responsibility from the site.

Claiming more than one million pages of content, RipoffReport. com has tremendous authority with search engines and is the bane of online reputation management firms the world over. The site is run by Ed Magedson, who, if you believe an article on *Forbes*, lives a fearful life in a fortified compound in an undisclosed location in Arizona.[8] Why? RipoffReport.com lets anyone post negative information about people or businesses, and Magedson will never take it down. Consequently, he has many enemies.

On Fox News, Bill O'Reilly featured RipoffReport.com as one of the worst websites in America.[9] The site mints money while making the subjects of its reports miserable, and its victims get so pissed off that they—again, if you believe Magedson and *Forbes*—would kill Magedson if they passed him on the street.

Given all this, it still all comes down to Google. Online complaint sites remain in business because their complaints rank quickly and highly on search results on Google and other search engines. Most online complaint sites leave the complaints or posts up, even if the original authors want to take them down.

If these complaint sites seem to have limited overall value for the general public, and anyone can say whatever they want with no devotion to truth or accuracy, why would Google continue to give them value on search results?

Some experts believe it is all about advertising. Complaint sites serve as Google's advertising partners and drive traffic to Google sponsored ads. So despite the common assertion that Google advertising has nothing to do with search results, some folks say otherwise.

Just as complaining in general isn't going anywhere, neither are complaint sites.

Build a Reputational Firewall

On March 24, 2006, the news program *60 Minutes* aired a story about a famous yet secretive hedge fund billionaire Steven Cohen, who was embroiled in a stock-shorting lawsuit. While the story itself was interesting, one thing that struck me was that *60 Minutes* didn't have a photograph of the famous trader. The background was that he had purchased the rights to every photo taken of him and actively prevented his image from being published anywhere. He was rarely seen in public and used private garages whenever he traveled in his chauffeured car. The only film that the news show could find was grainy security-camera footage of him exiting a hotel through a back entrance. Talk about managing one's image!

Sadly, the other 99.99 percent of us don't have the financial wherewithal to prevent unwanted images from being published online. We have to use other means to safeguard our online reputation. (Today, it is easy to find images of Cohen as he later embraced the media and public relations to bolster his overall image.) For businesses and individuals who might be prone to online criticism, there are other rules to live by.

Stake your claim to your name. This is really basic stuff but it merits repeating. In a crisis, it is important for your customers and the public to be able to hear your news as directly as possible from the source. Your company should have a Twitter account, a Facebook page, and a LinkedIn page if for no other reason than it verifies your company's identity and authenticates your news.

Address negative info. If there's negative information about your company posted online, you have to react in some way. Review sites generally enable companies to respond to comments, both positive and negative. Take advantage of this option. Damaging content can be addressed by online reputation management firms, which can push negative results lower on the search results page by publishing positive info to the web on your behalf. Such suppression tactics can be successful.

Another option is to put forth the extra effort to secure positive reviews from your happy customers. It can pay off in many ways.

For example, a few years ago my family visited South Carolina, and in advance we booked a trip on Adventure Harbor Tours, which at that time was the number-one rated attraction on TripAdvisor in Charleston. We arrived for our tour and learned that the boat taking us to see Fort Sumter and Morris Island was an 18-foot open fishing boat with seats for about 10. The captain and his crew were fantastic and led my family on a great morning of sightseeing and hunting for shark's teeth. (Yes, you can find shark's teeth in Charleston Harbor—the captain practically guarantees it.)

As we pulled into the dock on the return trip, Captain Howie asked us to rate his company on TripAdvisor if we had a good time. When we returned to our hotel that night, my kids happily complied. A few summers later we returned to find that Captain Howie had bought another boat for his fleet—the new one was more than double the size and accommodated 30 guests. Captain Howie, who is not my client but will be happy to read this, has hundreds of positive reviews, which not only drive business but also drown out the few negative ones. As of this writing, Adventure Harbor Tours remains one of the top-rated outdoor activities in Charleston.

Build your online firewall. If your business could be hijacked by negative reviews and online attacks, then you need to ensure that you regularly publish your positive news and build a legacy of positive internet results. It's tougher for negative information to take center stage in the future if there's already a lot of positive information anchoring top search results.

When a piece of negative material or bad opinion appears, you need to address it in some manner. You may choose to let it ride, but thoughtful consideration should win out.

Businesses Facing Online Attacks

If your business is hit with negative online content, the key is to make a careful assessment and determine the proper course of action. A hasty online reaction rarely helps, and most angry responses will only make things worse. In many instances, understanding the site where the post was published has as much impact on the strategy as the actual content of the post. A response of any kind may actually harm your chances of having an item removed later on, so it pays to be deliberate.

Overall assessment. Review the online issue and determine if this is a one-time issue or if it has the chance to become an ongoing and long-term problem. A one-time occurrence such as a blog post, forum post, or comment that is written by one person may be managed with a removal strategy. However, if an online post has already been widely shared and is appearing on multiple sites, then removal might be out of the question. Also, if a number of individuals are posting on an online complaint site or a review site, then a combination of engagement, removal, and suppression may be required. At this stage, it is also important to look at the overall impact of a negative online posting on your business. Is it impacting sales or impeding the sales process? The economic damage of a negative post should be assessed as it plays a role in the budget and plan for your strategy and future tactics.

Website assessment. Many websites and review sites will take information down if you make the request in the right way and with the right tone. If an individual can be convinced to remove a negative post, sites like Facebook, Twitter, LinkedIn, Yelp, and TripAdvisor enable the user to easily delete or modify a post. Personal websites, corporate websites, and blogs can also be altered by the user—the author may not want to, but it is technically possible. Other sites like bona fide news sites and online complaint sites will not alter their content. Such outlets will stand behind their right to free speech. News websites believe it is part of their rights as journalists. Complaint sites do it to make money.

Assess the author. In some cases, the source of the negative information is known. Posts on social media typically identify the author, as do most online reviews. If the author is known to the company, can they be contacted in order to resolve a pending customer-service issue and then be asked to take down the negative post? Is this just a person who needs some attention?

If the poster is anonymous, then it may be possible to find out their identity through legal channels. In such a case, it may take several months of working with web hosting companies and analyzing IP addresses to identify an anonymous poster. In some cases, just losing the veil of anonymity and a flash of legal muscle can compel a previously unknown person to remove a negative post.

Is the poster incredibly disgruntled or riding the crazy train? In some cases, you know who is posting negative information, and it's a lost cause. For example, you may have a customer who is so upset about their treatment that no number of apologies or "make-goods" will be enough. Other situations arise where negative information is posted by individuals who are mentally unstable or who get some level of joy from the fight. Engagement of any kind likely won't work in these situations.

Will it blow over? A typical reaction to negative online comments and postings is to try to ride it out. The online world moves fast and news can quickly move off of the front page. Part of the assessment phase has to involve whether or not an online posting has staying power. A negative story posted on a social media site may get views within the first few days but then fade from memory over a short period of time. When an online crisis hits, it is often best to make a measured assessment to see if negative online coverage gets traction with search engines. This may take a few days or a few weeks. Many business owners choose to live with the short-term blemish, figuring that a problem will eventually blow over.

Assess removal or de-listing by the host website. Some negative information can be taken down or de-listed from search results if you know who to ask. First, some sites have policies in place to de-list content if it meets certain criteria. For example, one of our clients had information about an embarrassing court case posted on a private legal research website. We analyzed the website and learned that the site would de-list a case published on the site if the matter was not precedent-setting and met some other requirements. We asked nicely and the embarrassing item was removed from search results. Second, some sites will remove negative information if it was posted by a third party and doesn't really belong on the site. In such cases, you may find a procedure already in place to enable removal, or a sensible and polite request made to the site owner or webmaster may be honored. Lastly, some sites, particularly online complaint sites, have procedures in place to mediate or request removal of negative posts, usually involving a fee. Read the fine print of such systems to ensure that they are indeed fair and free of bias.

For negative blog posts, look for violations of terms and conditions at the hosting level for sites like Blogger and Tumblr, but don't be surprised if the blog platform is non-responsive or rejects your pleas. Hiring an expert might make sense as those with experience with blog sites usually have better success getting negative blog posts removed or de-listed.

Get legal? If a post is truly defamatory, a legal strategy may work. Many law firms have experience with such matters, but beware that the wheels of justice turn slowly. I'm not a lawyer but the threat of legal action may convince a person to take down a negative post.

Engagement. Engagement of negative posts is a double-edged sword. Search engine optimization professionals typically say that engaging the publisher of negative information will only strengthen the post's online authority, potentially pushing it up search results. I tend to agree with this but with a few exceptions. First, some folks who post negative information primarily want a resolution to a business issue. So if they publish negative information on a social media site that enables them to modify or delete the post, then reaching out to them offline might get a satisfactory result for both parties. Second, engagement on online review sites is a standard best practice. Visitors to review sites want businesses to interact with their customers and see that problems are resolved.

Online complaint sites are a different beast. Engagement on a site like RipoffReport.com will only build online authority of the negative post. The owner of RipoffReport.com has said publicly that he will not remove posts, and users do not have the option to remove or edit their posts. On sites like this, the playing field is not level, and traditional tactics generally won't work. In addition, some legal strategies to attempt to get RipoffReport.com items de-listed from Google results hinge on whether or not the victim knows the poster. If you engage on RipoffReport.com, you may hurt your chances of securing a de-listing through the court system.

Sorry, you might be screwed—but not completely. Some online problems can't be fixed. I hate to admit it, but some nightmares won't go away, except if given time and if you hit them with multiple strategies. If you have a ton a negative stories online about your company, no single strategy will work to solve the problem as it will likely take some combination of suppression, review management, and targeted removals—and time.

The same can be said of negative stories on major news websites. It is nearly impossible to get articles removed from top-tier news sites or to have such articles de-listed from search results. I don't say completely impossible because I have seen some individuals have success asking a news website to de-index articles that were personally damaging—but only after multiple requests and only under the best of circumstances.

Lastly, if you are the victim of a high profile social media gaffe or instance of online shaming, then sadly, such things may never disappear or drop from search results. What we don't know but can hope for is that Google's ever-evolving algorithm will give less weight to social media missteps in the future and let time heal some of these wounds.

Some folks advertise removals. If you search Google for companies that advertise a service to remove negative content, such as reviews found on online complaint sites, you will find a wide range of folks offering such services. For example, you may be told that for a few thousand dollars, a company can get stories taken down from complaint sites or gossip sites. This is typically a back-channel, pay-for-play move where a third party is asking the complaint site to remove the negative content for a fee. To some, it looks and feels like you are paying an extortion fee. Playing in this mucky playground can be a sketchy proposition as they may be scamming you or selling a suppression strategy masked as a removal.

My advice is to look for a company that will do the work on a contingency basis and offer you some level of guarantee—say, for a period of a year. Then you need to make the leap of faith and sign an agreement that states you will pay the fee upon successful removal from the site or successful de-listing from Google. And then, when they are successful, make sure you pay their fees—as you are probably dealing with folks who can do further damage to you if you don't pay their bill. Scammers exist, so it is best to deal with reputable companies that are based in the United States (or your home country) and don't require money up front—unless they are charging you for very specific deliverables that are not contingency based.

Covert ops. In recent years, a secretive cottage industry has emerged comprising online reputation specialists who know how to make some results disappear from search results. Using a combination of skills, including a deep understanding of how websites work and how terms and conditions are enforced, these experts can successfully get some search results either removed from websites or de-listed from search results—regardless of whether the content is true, defamatory, or indifferent. The tactics are legal, sophisticated, and expensive. Some specialists will charge $10,000–$20,000 to remove a single link from search results. If you choose to engage someone in this realm, work with a reputable company, ensure that payment is only made on a contingency basis, and ask for a guarantee that the link in question will not return for at least one year.

Consider the kitchen sink and hunker down for a long haul. For crisis situations when your company is bombarded with negative search results, the only viable solution may be to employ a number of strategies and tactics, including suppression, review management, and targeted removals as well media placements and other traditional tools offered by public relations and strategic communications professionals. And sadly, one can't expect a quick fix. When dealing with tough cases, it may take several months or even a year or more to clean up results—and some issues may never get resolved to the satisfaction of a business owner.

The Deep Web and Online Reputation

Most of this book discusses online issues as they relate to search engines and how the majority of us view information on the internet. We begin most of our online interactions through a search engine like Google or Bing or we access information directly through mobile apps associated with Facebook, CNN, the Weather Channel, or another organization that makes its offerings easily reachable. This part of the internet, which everyone can see and is indexed by search engines, is known as the surface web and sometimes called the clear web or visible web.

However, vast amounts of information and data are exchanged out of the sight of search engines. Known as the deep web, this area includes dynamic web pages, blocked sites, unlinked sites, private sites (like those that require login credentials), non-HTML content, and private networks. Some estimates suggest the amount of information on the deep web (also known as the deep net, invisible web, or hidden web) is 500 times greater than the surface web. Within the deep web resides another area of the internet called the dark web (also known as the dark net), where individuals can exchange information anonymously, and oftentimes do so nefariously.

To recap, the surface web includes most of the websites that people view on search engines. The deep web comprises everything that is on the internet but isn't indexed or can't be indexed by search engines. The dark web is an area of the deep web where people search and exchange information anonymously. The dark web is part of the deep web, but the deep web is not necessarily dark. And it's inaccurate to suggest that all information on the deep web is deliberately clandestine or malicious.

Most frequently, people compare the internet to an iceberg and describe the surface web as the ice above the water and the deep web as the 90 percent of the ice you can't see beneath the waterline. Information on the deep web and dark web can have a tremendous impact on online reputation, so it's important to understand the differences.

A Primer on the Deep Web

Huge amounts of information are currently located on the deep web. If you have a website and choose to de-index a page from search results, then that page becomes a part of the deep web. If you have a password protected website, then the pages behind your login entrance are on the deep web. Included there all of the stories behind paywalls on news websites like The *Wall Street Journal*, all of the movies on Netflix, files in the cloud on sites like Dropbox, your e-mails, subscription databases, and all of your online banking records. All of this data, for the most part, is moving throughout the internet safely, securely, and without issue.

On one of my websites, for example, I have a client checklist that resides on a de-indexed page. If I want a client to access it, I simply send them the link and they can download the checklist. It can't be found on Google, because it isn't indexed, but it is accessible on the deep web. In some cases, you can access the deep web by conducting a search within a particular website.

However, the key problem with the deep web is that information from a company can be purposely or inadvertently posted there, and a business owner may not know it. For example, if a person at your company were to accidentally publish a list of your employees' home phone numbers on your company website on a typical indexed page, that page would likely find its way to the search engines within a few days. As the business owner, you might start to get some angry phone calls and e-mails from unhappy co-workers very soon afterward—as their private information is now publicly accessible for anyone who has access to a search engine.

Yet if that same list were to be published on a de-indexed page on your site, then the list would reside on the deep web, invisible to the search engines, but still accessible to folks who know how to search the deep web.

Many businesses have information on the deep web they that don't even know about. It's hidden, either on purpose or by accident, from the average web surfer. And such information can cause issues. What if an employee accidentally posted all of a restaurant's recipes to a de-indexed page that he thought was inaccessible because it wasn't visibly linked to the company website or found on a search engine? What if a list of client contact information was uploaded to a company website by an employee or vendor who inaccurately believed it to be secure? Such information, in the wrong hands, could cause irreparable damage to a business.

The next question is, how do you access information that is online but not found by search engines? Enter very smart people, hackers, and other assorted wonks. Data privacy experts as well as data pirates use special search terms and search strings to precisely look for deep web information that might cause a business to be vulnerable.

In fact, a 200-page document called "The Pirate's Code" lists thousands of search strings that can be used to scour the deep web for files that meet specific criteria. For example, search strings can look for deep web documents that are specifically labelled "top secret" or "confidential" or search for files with usernames, passwords, or e-mail addresses. Specific searches for resumes or Microsoft Outlook data files can be conducted. Again, thousands of search strings have been created to try to root out data and information that a business or individual may not want to be public.

To be honest, most of the search strings in "The Pirate's Code" look like gibberish to me, but cybersecurity experts say that this information represents the keys to the kingdom. On the deep web, cybersecurity and online reputation become interconnected. More on this a bit later.

Understanding the Dark Web

The dark web comprises part of the deep web, but it is distinctly different and much scarier. Individuals use the dark web to communicate anonymously. While some privacy advocates say it is their absolute right to not be tracked online, others use it specifically for crime.

On the dark web, individuals can find sources of illegal drugs, counterfeit money, weapons, leaked documents, and child pornography among other illicit things. It is also used by underground groups, dissidents, and whistleblowers—and journalists who wish to communicate with them. Law enforcement and government agencies also search the dark web to track criminals and terrorists. Again, it can be a scary place.

When you hear stories about millions of stolen credit card numbers, healthcare records being hacked and sold, or individuals being arrested for possessing child pornography, the information was most likely exchanged on the dark web. Transactions are done anonymously, and virtual currency like Bitcoin is the preferred form of payment.

WARNING: I'm going to explain how the dark web works on a rudimentary level, but I don't recommend that you check it out. In my opinion, the dark web is like a bad neighborhood that you don't want to visit at night. Not much good can come from it unless you are looking for something illegal. Again, this is my opinion, and some internet purists, privacy advocates, and conspiracy theorists probably disagree.

Access to the dark web requires a special web browser, of which there are several. You can't get there from the search bar on Chrome, Safari, internet Explorer, or Firefox. So don't worry that your toddler will find their way to it while playing games on an iPad. Your teenaged children? That's another story.

One of the most well-known browsers for the dark web is called Tor. It originally stood for "The Onion Router" as its many layers of encryption are akin to an onion. Today it is just called Tor, and it serves as an open-source software program that allows users to protect their privacy and security. Ironically, Tor was originally developed for the U.S. Navy as a way to protect government communications.

Tor is made up of a group of volunteer-operated servers that enable people to communicate privately and confidentially using a series of virtual tunnels and connections. On its website, Tor bills itself as a tool with many above-board uses:

- Individuals use it as an effective censorship circumvention tool, a mechanism for maintaining civil liberties online, and a place for socially sensitive communication: chat rooms, and web forums for crime and abuse survivors or people with illnesses.
- Journalists use Tor to communicate more safely with whistleblowers and dissidents.

- Non-governmental organizations use it to enable their workers to connect to their home website while they're in a foreign country, without revealing their location.

- Corporations use it as a safe way to conduct competitive analysis and to protect sensitive communications from eavesdroppers.

- Law enforcement uses Tor for visiting or surveilling websites without revealing government IP addresses and for security during sting operations.

Once you download and install the Tor browser, you can begin the process of searching anonymously and seek out dark web forums and sites with all manners of information. A search of the surface web for dark web links can serve as a guide. (If you click a dark web link from a surface web browser such as Chrome, you will get an error message.)

For example, a quick surface web search for dark web links led me to an entry called "What are some cool dark websites?" On this page was a long list of dark web links for gaming, politics, cryptography, education, crime, cats, and so on. It also included a warning: "Some of these definitely contain adult content, disturbing content, or possibly illegal activity (i.e., drug markets, gun markets, hacking services, etc.). Don't go walking in like, 'Hey everybody!! Can I get some coke and grenades??'" [10]

So why does this matter? I'm not a cybersecurity expert, and I don't hang out on the dark web. However, I do believe that many companies, particularly large enterprises that have significant amounts of data, should be monitoring the deep web and its dark web neighborhood.

I spoke with Brook Zimmatore of brand protection agency Massive, and he told me that many companies are vulnerable to deep web issues that are frequently of their own doing. His company has developed software to search the deep web and dark web for security threats on behalf of the firm's clients.

Deep web searches often turn up sales documents, sensitive corporate information, copies of confidential agreements, social media account login information, and so on. His firm has even found damaging information such as documents detailing unethical sales practices, confidential legal settlements, and even the complete blueprints of a company's security architecture. All of this information was found on the deep web, just below the surface but not behind a login or any security firewall. It was placed there, either purposely or inadvertently, and the companies had no clue.

According to Zimmatore, if this type of information ends up in the hands of a threat actor or bad guy, a company could be damaged on both the financial and reputational fronts. Cybersecurity and reputation management are blood brothers.

For example, when 40 million credit card numbers were stolen from retail giant Target in late 2013, it was a cybersecurity breach of never-before-seen proportions. When news of the theft was announced, Target took a tremendous reputational hit, on top of millions of dollars in operational costs. Once the dust settled, the data breach cost Target $162 million.[11] A similar breach in 2014 cost Home Depot $63 million.[12] Some of those costs went directly toward rebuilding the damaged reputation and trust between the retailers and their customers.

Problems discovered on the deep or dark web, which some may think are strictly of concern to the cybersecurity department, can quickly become issues for the public relations, communications, and customer service divisions—and the C-suite.

According to Zimmatore, every business should have a deep web strategy, particularly financial institutions, publicly traded companies, retailers, educational institutions, healthcare companies, and any large enterprise that touches private information. Even if you don't have millions of credit card numbers winding through your servers, you could be vulnerable to a threat found on the deep web.

Business Owner Online Reputation Checklist

- Monitor search engines including Google, Bing, and Yahoo for mentions of your company name, brands, products, and the names of your key executives. Establish a systemized approach using Google alerts, for example, or monitoring software.

- Monitor social media sites for mentions of your company, its brands, your products, and the names of key executives. This should include Facebook, Twitter, Instagram, Pinterest, and others. Google alerts may not catch these so it is best to monitor the individual feeds or investigate monitoring software.

- Claim your company profiles on top review sites like Yelp, TripAdvisor, Glassdoor, Angie's List, and others. Claiming the profile enables a business to be alerted of new reviews and promotes engagement. If a company profile is unclaimed, then the company's image on that site is left completely in the hands of the reviewers. Review sites can also be a source of new business leads.

- Review your company website for deep web threats. Some companies may have publicly accessible information posted on their website that is not visible to search engines. A regular review of deep web vulnerabilities can prevent potential online damage.

- Establish a social media policy so that employees understand how they should and should not behave on social media sites. The policy should address confidentiality issues, request that employees use good judgment when posting, and remind them that they do not speak on behalf of their employers. A sample can be found on page 108.

- Establish a media policy regarding inquiries from reporters and journalists. Members of the media may reach out to employees over social media channels, and employers need to remind workers and colleagues that they are not authorized to speak with the media on behalf of the organization. A sample can be found on page 112.

- Develop plans and procedures to respond to online inquiries and comments. Questions, comments, and feedback received through social media channels should be addressed in a systematic manner.

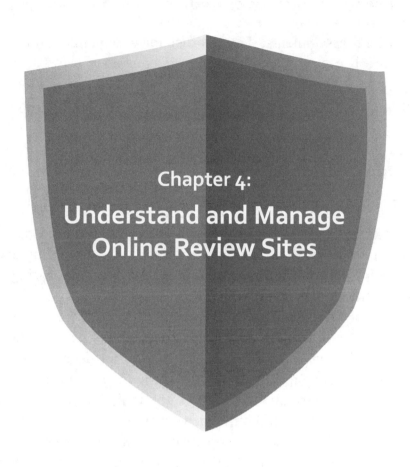

Chapter 4:

Understand and Manage Online Review Sites

"What have you done to us by creating Yelp? All of us are critiquing each other all the time. Would you like to apologize?"

—Stephen Colbert questioning Yelp co-founder and CEO Jeremy Stoppelman on *The Late Show with Stephen Colbert*, January 12, 2016.

How often do you say or hear questions such as these: How was the food at the new restaurant? What did you think of the hotel in New York? How was the new Muppets movie? Today, online reviews impact businesses far more than newspaper critics or rating organization assessments. The internet made it possible for us to review nearly every business and put the consumer at the controls. Crowd-sourced reviews have a major impact on online reputation.

Human beings like to review things. Food and restaurant reviewers date back to the early 1800s, and I imagine music critics predate *Rolling Stone Magazine* by a thousand years. We are predisposed to offer reviews, but prior to the internet, we had limited means to broadcast them. Interestingly, the preeminent review entity from my youth and young adulthood was *Consumer Reports*, a then-magazine and now-magazine-plus-website that offers objective ratings of all manners of consumer products. The cool thing about *Consumer Reports* has always been that it accepts no advertising and buys the products that it reviews. For example, *Consumer Reports* will buy every brand of dishwasher and then run them through a battery of tests in order to rate them on durability, value, efficacy, and so on. *Consumer Reports* was sought after for decades because of its independence and objectivity. Printing costs and limitations in information distribution prevented any real challengers. In my opinion, in a perfect world, all reviews would be like those offered by *Consumer Reports*: honest, objective, and unencumbered by the wishes of advertisers and sponsors. Unfortunately, that's not the case.

As an aside, my father has always been a diehard researcher and frequently would tell my brothers and me about the best cars, televisions, clothes washers, etc., as determined by *Consumer Reports*. We drew the line when he arrived at a family gathering with cheap beer that had scored highly with *Consumer Reports*—sometimes brand must trump test-kitchen quality.

The New Normal

Today, online review sites do not have the same non-profit mission as *Consumer Reports*. Sites like Yelp, TripAdvisor, Glassdoor, and Angie's List are distinctly for-profit entities. Most are either owned by publicly traded companies or rising venture-capital funded organizations with their eyes on the bottom line. I refer to these organizations as review "sites" as in "websites," but they are typically more than that as mobile apps play an ever-increasing role in online reviews.

So how did this happen? I already mentioned that, as a species, we like to review things and pass judgment. The smart executives at these sites have figured this out, even if somewhat by accident, and built on this by expanding their offerings, enabling businesses to participate on the sites for free (and for pay), and by offering ways for companies to grow their businesses my maximizing online reviews.

It has actually become very difficult to find objective online reviews as many wholesalers and distributors of products have taken to the internet to sell their wares and bought up and built out website domain names that appear to be review sites like *Consumer Reports* but are, in fact, search optimized sites designed to drive traffic to a particular brand or a particular distributor. Search engine optimization companies have taken advantage of our desire for objective information and now push us to sites that are not in the least objective. This has helped create opportunities for the major review sites.

The value proposition for a review site is simple. It enables almost anyone to offer a public review and rating of a business. If a restaurant has great food at affordable prices, a customer can go online and slather the restaurant with praise. Conversely, if a hotel's website suggests it is a luxury property right on the ocean but is, in fact, a bit dumpy and two blocks from the water, a guest can visit a review site and warn future customers of the hotel's failure to meet expectations. Further, if a customer has a particularly bad experience with a plumber, painter, or roofer, then he can visit a review site and unleash his frustration with prose, poetry, or another form of venomous invective.

By offering these options to consumers, review sites have grown in popularity and built impressive online authority. For example, if you type the name of your city and the word "restaurant" into the Google search bar, you will more than likely find listings from Yelp and TripAdvisor on page one. If you type your city and the word "plumber" into the search bar, you will likely get listings from Angie's List and Yelp on the first two pages. And if you type the name of your company and the word "jobs" into a search engine, you will likely find reviews from the site Glassdoor on the first two pages of results. Even further, for many companies, particularly those in hospitality, TripAdvisor and Yelp reviews may appear as the first or second listing on Google results—and they often outperform the hotel's or restaurant's own website.

As these sites grow in popularity, their authority with search results will only increase. The more companies participate on the sites, the bigger the sites become and the more their authority grows. The impact is building. As one review site executive said to me, "The genie is out of the bottle." Review sites are here, they are dominating search results, and they can't be ignored.

A New Equation

For business owners, review sites have become a part of their marketing equation, whether they like it or not. PowerReviews, a provider of ratings, reviews, and question-and-answer technology to global brands and retailers, surveyed consumers in 2014 and published an interesting study.[1] Among its findings are the following:

- ❤ The top five factors impacting purchasing decisions (in order) are (1) price, (2) ratings and reviews, (3) recommendation from friends and family, (4) brand, and (5) free shipping and retailer.

- ❤ Ratings and reviews have become a major source of information for shoppers as a whopping 95 percent of consumers in the study reported consulting customer reviews. Of those shoppers, 24 percent consult reviews for every purchase they make. For shoppers 18–44, that number jumps to 30 percent.

- All consumers rely on the presence of negative reviews for authenticity and credibility.

- Because consumers want to be confident in their purchases, the availability of product reviews is an important factor in their decision for big-ticket purchases such as electronics (82 percent), appliances (80 percent), and computers (80 percent).

- 70 percent of mobile shoppers reported being more likely to purchase a product if the mobile site or app they're purchasing from has reviews.

- Ratings and reviews have become table stakes, and brands and retailers can improve consumer experience with reviews.

- By making it easy for consumers to read and write reviews at home, in-store, or on the go, brands and retailers increase traffic and conversions.

From my analysis of the study results and its accompanying report, it's clear that reviews continue to grow in importance for both consumers and businesses. In addition, consumers don't expect a business to be perfect, so they anticipate that some companies will have a small amount of negative feedback. Lastly, just as mobile search has overtaken desktop search, I expect mobile usage of these review organizations may already or will soon outpace desktop usage.

Unfortunately, the growth of review sites likely means businesses must dedicate resources to manage online reviews. The plus side is that review sites can drive new business and also improve your company's reputation with customers as well as potential employees.

Why do people leave reviews? A common perception among business owners is that customers only visit review sites to complain. Some research suggests otherwise. Early in its existence, back in 2007, travel review site TripAdvisor worked with tourism professor Dr. Ulrike Gretzel to research what motivates travelers to leave reviews. Here's a salient point from the study: "Online travel review writers are mostly motivated by a concern for other consumers, helping a travel service provider and needs for extraversion/positive self-enhancement. Venting negative feelings or receiving rewards for postings are not seen as important motives."[2]

According to Dr. Gretzel's findings, people leave reviews because they want to help other consumers and assist the property, restaurant, or attraction and because seeing their review published makes them feel good. Blasting a hotel or restaurant about bad service is not a primary motivator.

Executives at review sites are quick to point out that most online reviews are, in fact, positive and that their sites are building an overall sense of community—not just providing a venue for bashing. However, it is unmistakable that negative reviews cause anxiety for businesses, can lead to losses in revenue, and cause reputational damage. Specific guidance on several high profile sites follows in this chapter, but after completing interviews with executives from several review sites including Yelp, TripAdvisor, and Glassdoor, I can offer some general recommendations for managing online reviews.

Face this new reality. Review sites are here to stay, so we can't put our heads in the sand and ignore them anymore. Sites exist to review all manners of businesses, and your business may have reviews that you have never seen—leaving the reputation of your business in the hands of the internet community without any input from the business owner or management. Review sites have strong authority with search engines, and online reputation management firms that have attempted to suppress review sites with positive content are losing the battle. Many online reputation pros have thrown in the towel and are now recommending engagement to change what review sites say, rather than trying to push them down in search results. It's time to join party.

Claim or create your company page on the main review sites. As I have said before, you don't get to be off the grid. Your company may not yet have a listing on a site like Yelp, but any customer or interested party could create one without your knowledge and certainly without your consent. Business owners should look at the main review sites and either claim their page if one has already been created or create their own listing—this will give you a small level of control. If you have a claimed page, then you can enable the tools provided to businesses by review sites, such as notifications of new reviews and the ability to respond to reviews. This is the single most important reason to claim your page, so that you will be notified of new reviews.

Build out your review site listings. Across the board, executives from review sites recommend completing profiles and adding information to business listings. Up-to-date photos, videos, and descriptions increase page views as well as interest from prospective customers or employees. Plain listings without images look stale as customers on review sites are typically interested in getting current information. At a minimum, most review sites offer the opportunity to post photos, videos, detailed descriptions, hours of operations, and contact information.

Engagement. Likely the biggest trend in online reviews centers on engagement. Interaction between businesses and their customers helps build the overall sense of community, and executives from review sites universally advocate for responding to both positive and negative reviews. While responding to a negative review may not change the opinion of the reviewer, the response may positively impact the next consumer. According to TripAdvisor, for example, business owners should explain in responses how they plan to remedy negative situations. Future customers appreciate honesty and also react favorably to engaged businesses.

Another way that businesses can engage with review sites is by asking and encouraging customers for reviews. Most review sites view this as a key part of their community: The more the merrier. Sites such as TripAdvisor, Glassdoor, Google Reviews, and Angie's List want businesses to have many reviews as they view it as promotion for their sites—and it also adds to the overall size and depth of the respective sites, furthering their overall authority with search engines. Some sites also give more weight to newer reviews. The main exception to this is Yelp, which does not want its member companies to influence reviews in any way. This is a source of consternation among some businesses that I address in detail later in this section.

Responding to reviews remains a chief area of engagement, and in some instances, responses to negative reviews can actually generate positive attention. For example, a bar owner in New York City responded to the author of a one-star rating published on Yelp about his establishment, the Iron Horse. The reviewer said the bar was not a good place for a quiet drink and then posted the one-star rating. Owner Zbigniew Szymczyk thanked her for her visit, but then gave her a "review" of his own.[3]

He blasted the reviewer, his displeased customer, for not aligning her expectations with the place she was patronizing. The Iron Horse bills itself as a loud "dive" bar that sells $2 beers, despite its premium location. "We are primarily a loud, party type bar atmosphere, serving a mean burger, hot wings, and similar pub fare at RIDICULOUSLY low prices for Lower Manhattan," Szymczyk wrote on Yelp. He concluded, "I give you 1 star as you are terrible at finding bars and restaurants that suit your tastes."

Szymczyk's Yelp response was noticed by Eater.com and quickly went viral, appearing on many other websites and news outlets including The *New York Post, The Daily Mail* in the United Kingdom, and Mashable.com. I, for one, hope to visit the Iron Horse one day because I not only appreciate good wings and $2 beer but also to shake the hand of Szymczyk for appropriately and humorously engaging a negative reviewer.

Of course, I'm not saying that you should attack any person who offers a negative review, but engagement on review sites should be viewed as a conversation. If your company makes a mistake or offers lousy service, acknowledge it. At the same time, don't be afraid to engage negative reviewers who have stepped out of line.

Pay close attention for review blackmail. Some online reviewers are not nice people. Feeling slighted by their treatment at a hotel, restaurant, or other establishment, they reach out to the business with a threat such as "comp my room or I will write a negative online review." If you think this sounds like blackmail, you are correct because it is. Fortunately, several online review sites have policies in place to prevent this activity. If a negative review is threatened on TripAdvisor, for example, the site enables companies to reach out to the site, before a blackmail review is even posted, and let the TripAdvisor staff know of an impending threat. The site asks for some details on the situation, including the name of the reviewer and their e-mail address. A blackmail review can also be flagged by the company after the fact. In its content guidelines, Yelp prohibits asking for payment, beyond a refund, in exchange for modifying or deleting a review.

Don't try to fix "crazy." When speaking with one executive who has had tremendous success with Yelp, he mentioned that they have some very simple rules. His company will bend over backwards for his customers, but "we don't do crazy." Sometimes customers have outrageous expectations, and every business owner has dealt with clients who may not be "all there in the head." And amazingly, it seems like the internet is breeding such people. A business should be prepared to walk away from an online problem if the demands made by the customer go well beyond reason.

Yelp

Founded in 2004, online review site Yelp often confounds business owners. It is, without question, one of the dominant review sites and one that oftentimes outperforms company websites on search results. What that means is that a search for a particular restaurant on a search engine, for example, could pull up the Yelp review ahead of the restaurant's actual site. Now if the reviews on Yelp are positive, then this may increase the chance of a customer booking. However, the opposite may be true if reviews are largely negative.

A Harvard Business School study in 2011 found that each star in a Yelp rating impacted sales by between 5–9 percent.[4] Another study suggested that increasing a star rating from 3.5 to 4 on Yelp would increase a restaurant's chances of being booked during peak hours by 19 percent.[5]

Some businesses, such as those in case studies listed later in this chapter, have seen dramatic marketing results from actively working with Yelp and engaging the Yelp community. If managed correctly, the site has the potential to help generate business for companies with listings, but the site has some idiosyncrasies that need to be addressed and managed.

As a business, Yelp is another of the classic internet-created companies. Prior to sites like Yelp, many service businesses only marketed through personal referrals and Yellow Pages ads. But the internet, which democratized so many aspects of commerce, enabled companies like Yelp to tap into consumers directly and solicit first-hand reviews of all manners of companies from restaurants and hotels to roofers and locksmiths.

Yelp derives its revenue from advertising and business partnerships. While offering what it believes to be objective information about various types of businesses and service providers, it makes its money from sponsored posts and by earning commissions on certain types of transactions. Exactly when and how they get paid for these transactions is less important than knowing that they want the site to be as useful and densely packed with information as possible for its users. The site promotes engagement between businesses and its users as this makes the site denser but also keeps users on the site longer. It's the old website "stickiness" argument. If you keep visitors on your site longer, then they are more likely to click on your sponsored ads or use the services from which you derive revenue.

Yelp's content is provided exclusively by its users with curation by the site—primarily to eliminate fake reviews and limit the influence of reviews that the site managers believe are not legitimate. Yelp has developed an algorithm that, among other things, attempts to sniff out fake reviews as well as any it believes may not have been generated organically—more on that later as well.

Yelp wants its reviews to be genuine and unencumbered, so it works hard to prevent the publication of reviews that may have been faked in some manner. Yelp strives to be a grassroots site, and the company's executives are extremely cautious, perhaps overly, when it comes to attempts to manipulate reviews.

I spoke with Yelp's Director of Local Business Outreach Darnell Holloway to get some direct recommendations on how business owners can better work with Yelp. He offered some common-sense recommendations along with some other insider tips.

If You Can't Beat 'Em, Join 'Em

Yelp's first recommendation is that you "claim" your business page, and it's good advice. Remember, it's a fallacy to think that you can stay off the grid. If your page is "unclaimed," then your company's reputation on Yelp is completely in the hands of its users.

Claiming your page has practical advantages. Remember, Yelp wants you engaged, so the company offers a suite of free tools for every business listed on the site. While the site offers promotion opportunities, this main set of tools is free and available to companies both large and small.

By claiming your page, you can post your hours of operation, detailed directions, contact information, product information, menus, and so forth. It offers an opportunity to tell your company story (hopefully consistently and authentically) and, as Holloway points out, humanize your business. Again, it makes sense. If you are researching a business and compare listings between Company A, which has a bare bones listing, and Company B, which has in-depth information, photographs, and details about it latest offerings, which one has a better chance of earning a new customer? I'm going with B.

According to Holloway, consumers want to see that the experience that a company offers is in line with the reviews, so if the reviews suggest that a restaurant is a great place to watch the sunset, then doesn't it make sense that photographs provided by the business should feature rosy-fingered twilight images?

As important as it is to paint pictures of how phenomenal your business is, claiming your page also gives you the ability to have a small level of control of the actual online reviews. Claiming your page enables you to better monitor reviews as they come in and also reply publicly and/or privately to users who review your business. This aspect of engagement is critical. No greater reason exists to claim your business listing than to be notified of new reviews so that you can respond.

Use the Mobile App

Holloway's second big picture recommendation involves Yelp's mobile app. His recommendation to business owners is to get it and use it. Most business owners don't sit at their desk all day, and in fact, some don't even have a desk anymore. We spend time out of the office, away from our desktops and only reachable via smartphones. Yelp recognizes this and created a mobile app that gives business owners access to its tools when on the road.

Here's a quick and simple tip that could help you make money with Yelp right away. Did you know that Yelp offers an option for users to request a quote through a business listing? And that this quote request can be sent directly to your phone via a texting feature? If you are in a business that requires quick responses to customer inquiries, then you could be missing out. And we all have to be exceptionally quick and nimble today, not just towing companies and the personal injury attorneys who follow them. Accessing Yelp via mobile device also puts you in more immediate touch should you wish to reply to a review.

That Pesky Algorithm and Yelp's Idea of Organic

The overall concept behind Yelp is very straightforward: Create a directory of businesses and offer a platform for customers to directly review those businesses. In a perfect world, all reviewers and business owners would be honest and forthright, and the best companies would be more highly rated than the worst companies.

Yet according to Yelp, fake reviews and attempts to game its system emerged shortly after the first iteration of its website launched. And Yelp cracked down. Authentic reviews are a cornerstone of any review site, and Yelp's idea of authenticity often puzzles business owners. Essentially, Yelp doesn't want business owners to influence reviewers or potential reviewers in any way that might bias the content.

So on one extreme, which is logical and reasonable, Yelp says that a business owner shouldn't review its own business nor should employees of a business write reviews of their employer's business— positive or negative. Yelp also outlaws schemes to pay reviewers or to make quid pro quo offers to potential reviewers. Such things would clearly bias reviews and undermine the review site. Following this logic, the site also outlaws reviews from competing businesses.

In addition, Yelp looks to prevent efforts to game its system. Early on, some Yelp member companies wanted to encourage customers to post reviews. At the time, it seemed like a good idea. For example, a car dealer sells a vehicle to a happy customer and just as he is handing over the keys he asks for a review on Yelp. The chipper new owners says yes and the salesman then sits the customer down at his computer and asks him to login to Yelp and post a review. Five brightly glowing stars later and all parties are happy, right? Not so fast. Yelp tracks IP addresses of reviewers and has trained its algorithm to look for patterns that it deems suspicious. Therefore, if a bunch of reviews, be them positive, negative, or indifferent, are posted from the same IP address, even if they are from different accounts, then Yelp may not publish them. Such reviews are biased, according to Yelp, even though the reviews may be accurate and represent the actual views of actual customers.

Yelp will also automatically analyze reviews against many other criteria. If a review is published from a computer that is not geographically close to the business, then it may be flagged by Yelp. This prevents a person in Maine from writing a review about a restaurant that they have never been to in Oregon. (Yes, I know there's probably a Portland joke in there somewhere.)

I pasted in the exact wording from the Yelp website below because not only does this represent what the Yelp algorithm screens against, but it also offers an idea of the leverage points a business owner might use to get a Yelp review taken down. More on that later, but first take a look at what Yelp discourages, and its rationale.[6]

Inappropriate content: Colorful language and imagery is fine, but there's no need for threats, harassment, lewdness, hate speech, and other displays of bigotry.

Conflicts of interest: Your contributions should be unbiased and objective. For example, you shouldn't write reviews of your own business or employer, your friends' or relatives' business, your peers or competitors in your industry, or businesses in your networking group. Business owners should not ask customers to write reviews.

Promotional content: Unless you're using your Business Owners Account to add content to your business's profile page, we generally frown upon promotional content. Let's keep the site useful for consumers and not overrun with commercial noise from every user.

Relevance: Please make sure your contributions are relevant and appropriate to the forum. For example, reviews aren't the place for rants about a business's employment practices, political ideologies, extraordinary circumstances, or other matters that don't address the core of the consumer experience.

Privacy: Don't publicize other people's private information. Please don't post close-up photos or videos of other patrons without their permission, and please don't post other people's full names unless you're referring to service providers who are commonly identified by or commonly share their own full names.

Intellectual property: Don't swipe content from other sites or users. You're a smart cookie, so write your own reviews and take your own photos and videos, please!

Demanding payment: Beyond simply asking for a refund to remedy a bad experience, you should not use removing or posting your review as a way to extract payment from a business, regardless of whether you've been a customer.

Some Reviews are More Equal Than Others

As you might imagine, Yelp has put a lot of responsibility on its algorithms to monitor reviews. It quickly must analyze reviews, weed out hate speech and private information, and then also attempt to judge reviewer intent. This is a difficult task that is far from perfect. A computer program decides, at least in the beginning, whether to publish or not publish a review.

Yet in a move that one could call either brilliant or dastardly depending on your perspective, Yelp has relieved some of the pressure of making what seems like a black or white decision by enabling its algorithm to place questionable reviews in a gray zone. While reviews that blatantly violate its rules may never get published, those in the gray zone are published to the site but are not recommended by Yelp.

Only recommended reviews count toward a business's overall star rating on Yelp. Reviews that are not recommended can still be viewed by Yelp users, but they are not displayed prominently. In some cases, a business might have dozens of positive reviews in the not recommended category but only one review that is recommended. If that one recommended review happens to be a one-star rating, then the entire business rating is listed as one star. This one-star rating then can end up listed very high on search results. I have seen this on several occasions, and it drives many business owners batty.

The Quest for Pure, Virginal Reviews

Yelp wants its reviews to be unbiased and completely authentic. While the site's executives want business owners to engage with the Yelp community, use its tools, advertise with them, and promote the site, Yelp does not want a business owner to ask its customers for reviews. Wait, what? Yes, Yelp wants engagement and it wants as many reviews as possible, but it wants such reviews to be completely free of any bias. I call this the quest for pure, virginal reviews. And this is likely at that heart of why some business owners look at Yelp with disdain.

You may have noticed this simple line from the content guidelines I posted above: "Business owners should not ask customers to write reviews." Here's the logic, and again, it's best to let Yelp's website break the news itself on this concept:[7]

> On Yelp, people read and write reviews about their favorite local businesses. So it might seem counter-intuitive that we actually discourage business owners from asking their customers to write reviews.

Why does Yelp discourage businesses from asking for reviews?

1. Would-be customers might not trust you. Let's face it, most business owners are only going to ask for reviews from their happy customers, not the unhappy ones. Over time, these self-selected reviews create bias in the business listing—a bias that savvy consumers can smell from a mile away. No business is perfect, and it's impossible to please 100% of your customers 100% of the time.

2. Solicited reviews are less likely to be recommended by our automated software, and that will drive you crazy. Why aren't these reviews recommended? Well, we have the unfortunate task of trying to help our users distinguish between real and fake reviews, and while we think we do a pretty good job at it with our fancy computer algorithms, the harsh reality is that solicited reviews often fall somewhere in between. Imagine, for example, the business owner who "asks" for a review by sticking a laptop in front of a customer and smilingly invites her to write a review while he looks over her shoulder. We don't need these kinds of reviews, so it shouldn't be a surprise when they aren't recommended.

Sounds good right? Pure, authentic, and transparent reviews rule the day, and we all walk off into the sunset hand-in-hand, singing show tunes. Such is not the case in the business world where I operate.

Here's a typical scenario. A business is merrily chugging along with little knowledge of sites like Yelp. Sure, the owner may have heard of the site and even used it to help choose a local hotel or restaurant but may have not imagined that his company would end up getting reviews on the site. One day, the business owner does a Google search and sees a Yelp listing on page one of search results, describing his business as a one-star entity. (Perhaps the Google search was prompted by noticing sales the previous month were a little soft.) A visit to Yelp shows a single negative review on an unclaimed page.

What does the business owner do next? Simple. He starts to research Yelp and tries to figure it out. Perhaps he knows the customer who posted the negative review and maybe not. Perhaps he thinks it's fake or from a competitor or disgruntled former employee. In all likelihood, the business owner does not believe the review is authentic and virginal. ("Virginal" is my characterization, not Yelp's. I use it to make a point.)

At this point, the business owner wants to take action. Remember, sales may be on the line. Yet if you follow Yelp's guidance, one should essentially do nothing. I will cover Yelp's official recommendations a bit later, but all options are very passive. I know very few successful business owners who choose passivity when their revenue is on the line. In most cases, the business owner wants the review taken down, and these efforts are almost always rebuffed by Yelp.

So the next option, again following entrepreneur logic, is to try to get some positive reviews. Business owners will invariably say that one negative review is not representative of their companies. However, if the business owner calls a bunch of his friends and asks them to review the company on Yelp, the flurry of new activity may be flagged by the Yelp algorithm. A burst of reviews from a group of first-time users will be seen as an attempt to game the site, and the prompted reviews won't be recommended. Yelp calls these first-time, one-time reviews "drive-by reviews," and its software is constantly looking for them.

In the situation described above, the business may continue to have one negative review in the recommended area and a handful of positive reviews in the not-recommended section. And sadly, the one-star image on Google persists. Scenarios like this, which are playing out across the Yelp universe, are at the heart of the Yelp conundrum that plagues many companies: One negative review can shape a company's image, and it is just not fair.

Here's another bit of insight into Yelp and how reviews get recommended or not. In order to write a review, a user must register on the site. Once you become a so-called Yelper, the site begins to track your activity, and your "value" as a user rises and falls depending on how engaged you are as a Yelper. Again, exactly how the algorithm works is proprietary, but users can increase their value on Yelp by completing their profile, adding photos of themselves, connecting with friends, and just using the site. A Yelp user can have a high value without ever posting a review to the site. Many users write reviews of businesses, but far more visit the site and the mobile app for information.

Another thing that drives business owners crazy is that a negative review that they see as killing their business is authored by a user who, based on their profile, hasn't reviewed many other companies. Yet the one review they have written, which is critical of their company, is recommended—and therefore killing their business. Yelp looks at the whole of a Yelper's activity, not just how many reviews have been published by that user.

If you want to play by Yelp's rules, there are ways to encourage more reviews—with the hope that new positive reviews will counterbalance any negative reviews. Yelp offers some subtle recommendations.

As we have learned, asking for a review is discouraged by Yelp, but the site does suggest that you tell your customers to "visit us on Yelp." To me, it's practically the same thing, but Yelp says otherwise. And as I will explain later, there may be consequences if Yelp catches you asking for reviews or trying to game the system.

To encourage customers to visit you, Yelp suggests adding Yelp window decals to your place of business, placing Yelp badges and counters on your website, and even adding Yelp logos to your e-mail signature. In addition, Yelp's Holloway suggests interacting with

Yelp by posting deals on your listing page including check-in offers and buy-one-get-one promotions. He also recommends activating reservation features on listings and using other Yelp tools to promote interaction. Such digital bread crumbs can encourage reviews.

Holloway also points out that most larger cities in the United States have Yelp employees on the ground called community managers. These folks organize events for Yelpers in the area and help promote engagement. Businesses that want to bring Yelpers to their location can work with community managers to create events to cater directly to Yelpers.

Use your Yelp-Given Talent for Good

The final piece of advice I gleaned from Holloway was to use the tools offered by Yelp to engage with your customers. He suggests viewing your company's relationship with Yelp as a tool to communicate with customers. View it as a means to have a conversation. Reply to reviews, both positive and negative. You can do this either publicly or privately. Upload photos of your business and its friendly employees. Use the quoting, reservation, and engagement features.

How to Deal With Negative Reviews

Contact the customer and ask them to modify it or take it down. The most straightforward way to manage a negative review on Yelp is to contact the customer and begin a conversation, either through a phone call, e-mail, or private message on Yelp. Find out where the problem lies and work to remedy it. Companies can then ask the reviewer to modify or delete a Yelp review after the issue has been resolved. This simple strategy has worked for many organizations and even turned negative reviews into positive ones. Unlike online complaint sites that promise to never take down reviews, bona fide online review sites like Yelp enable their users to modify or delete reviews.

Engage and comment. Regardless of whether a customer can be convinced to modify or delete a review, the business should publicly comment on the negative review and offer the company's side of the story. This humanizes the business and also shows future visitors to the site that the organization is concerned about negative feedback.

Flag it. Yelp enables business owners to flag reviews that violate its content guidelines or terms of service. Yelp will analyze flagged reviews and notify you of any action they have taken, and they may or may not reach out to the user.

Any user on Yelp can flag a review, as long as you are registered and logged in. In the lower right-hand corner of each review is a semi-transparent square with a little gray flag in it. When you hover over this square, you are given the option to report the review. When you click on it, it takes you to the "report review" screen, which offers a drop-down menu with the following options to report the review:

- It contains false information.
- It was posted by someone affiliated with the business.
- It was posted by a competitor, or ex-employee.
- It contains threats, lewdness, or hate speech.
- It doesn't describe a personal consumer experience.
- It violates Yelp's privacy standards.
- It contains promotional material.
- It's for the wrong business.

As exciting as it may be to click on the "it contains false information" link with hope that you will be able to plead your case regarding a negative review, Yelp quickly stops you in your tracks. The "it contains false information" option is not really an option at all. It's a dead end, offering this explanation when you click it:[9]

> *Sorry, but we don't take sides in factual disputes. If a review appears to reflect a user's personal experience and*

opinions, it is our policy to let the user stand behind their review.

There's always more than one side to a story, and business owners can address misunderstandings via their Business Account by posting a public comment or sending a private message to the reviewer.

When clicking drop-down menus for the other options, Yelp gives you the opportunity to explain why you believe the review is in violation of its rules. Yelp will then investigate and typically get back to you by e-mail in a few days.

My experience with flagging content on Yelp has been mixed. During my research for a presentation, I was reviewing the un-claimed Yelp listing of a company owned by a friend of mine. His company had a single one-star review, so I chose to investigate it. It turned out that the negative review was written by a lady who had seen one of the company's trucks and didn't like the company logo and the overall appearance of the truck. She was not a customer of his company but rather a third party who thought his vehicles were ugly.

I flagged this review on my friend's behalf because it did not "de-scribe a personal consumer experience." A few days later, Yelp took it down. I called my friend, telling him to claim his page and letting him know that some people are harsh critics of logos.

In another case, I learned of a jewelry store that was dealing with a negative review from a customer who was walking the line between being disgruntled and blackmail. The jeweler felt the cus-tomer was unreasonable in his pricing expectations, and the two sides were unable to make a deal. The customer left the store empty-handed and then chose to vent his frustrations on Yelp. When the store owner called the customer to see if they could resolve the situation and then take down the review, the customer would not budge on his unreasonable price request—essentially saying that he wanted his price or the negative review stayed online. To me, this is online blackmail and in violation of Yelp's guidelines. Sadly, Yelp felt otherwise, and the negative review remains.

Unfortunately, I have heard many stories from business owners who are frustrated with Yelp, particularly after they have made attempts to secure positive Yelp reviews. As we have learned, this is strictly forbidden by Yelp, and the business owners typically say they feel that they have been blackballed by Yelp, as very few positive reviews reach recommended status and negative reviews rule the day.

And my contacts are not alone. In 2010, several businesses challenged Yelp in court, saying that the site exchanges positive ratings for advertising dollars. Some of them even got together and attempted to make a documentary film that was to be titled *Million Dollar Bully*. It doesn't appear that they actually made the movie, but they did film a trailer that you can watch on YouTube. The trailer suggests that Yelp manipulates its recommended reviews to benefit advertisers, and one restaurant owner even compares the site to a certain kind of family business popularized by fictional characters Micheal Corleone and Tony Soprano. Several class action lawsuits were filed against Yelp, and it is important to note that all of them were dismissed in the U.S. Court of Appeals for the Ninth Circuit on September 2, 2014. Ironically, Yelp has an image problem among a number of its users.

Try to Game the System

While many war stories about Yelp end with companies lamenting losing the battle and ending up feeling defeated, some business have successfully outwitted Yelp's filters and algorithms. Discussing Yelp with a business owner I know, he said that he successfully rammed through some reviews by doing the following:

- He asked his employees to join Yelp, actively use the site, and publish reviews of other businesses for a period of at least a month.

- ● After the month, he told them to review his company with a four- or five-star review that was at least 300 words.

- ● He instructed them not to be "over the top" with their praise and to only post the review about the company after they had been active for several weeks.

Within a few months, his company had a handful of new positive reviews that counteracted some of the negative ones. This procedure, which violates almost all of Yelp's prime directives, proved effective. I'm not advocating this procedure, but it's an example of how entrepreneurs have little interest in passively accepting negative reviews and meekly waiting for pure, organic reviews to materialize and sail past Yelp's filters.

According to Yelp's Holloway, the site is continually working with business owners to educate them on how to best work with Yelp. The site offers free webinars every other week and has a searchable support area, and he says that if you call the inbound sales team, you can likely get a question answered.

For more information, visit *www.yelp.com/support*.

Case Study

Hard-Luck Animal Lover Becomes
New York City's Top Yelp Locksmith

By his own admission, Jay Sofer wasn't a great businessman. In 2008, he was doing contract work as a freelance locksmith in New York City and barely getting by. Two companies who regularly hired him had gone out of business, he lost his apartment, and he didn't have any money to further his education.

"I was on the wrong side of 20 and living in my mother's garage," says Sofer. Then a friend suggested he look into promoting himself online through sites like Craigslist and Yelp.

Sofer created a Yelp page for his company, LockBusters, with his contact information along with a few pictures of himself with his pets. A dedicated animal lover, his page has more photos of dogs than of deadbolts, doorknobs, or keys. Looking back on it, he realizes that he was showcasing himself as a real person on Yelp, and that made all the difference.

Soon business started to pick up, and within six months, Sofer was the top-rated locksmith in New York City, according to Yelp. "I didn't even know I had a lot of reviews," says Sofer. "I would go to the library to use a computer to check the Yelp site and saw that I was the highest-rated locksmith, and I was getting work from Yelp every day." Sofer believes Yelp enabled him to be competitive in a tough market, leveling the playing field for a small one-man shop.

Speaking with Sofer, you quickly learn that Yelp alone did not make him a success. He's personable and genuine and likes what he does. He answers his own phone, goes above and beyond for his customers, and tries to help them in any way he can. He believes Yelp has helped him offer a "small-town feel" to a crazy city like New York. "Customers visit my listing on Yelp and see that I'm a real person," he says. "When they call, they ask for me by name."

Sofer checks his Yelp site each day and regularly receives messages sent directly through the site. For every customer who posts a review, he replies either publicly or privately. And when the rare negative review comes in, he says he goes into "five alarm mode."

When a customer is unhappy, he does whatever he can to fix it. He goes back to the job site, stays as long as necessary, and does everything he can to make things right.

In fact, he candidly admits that his 100th review on Yelp came from remedying a screw up. He revisited an unhappy customer and fixed the problem. The client later gave him a five-star review, saying that she grew up in a small town and that Sofer gave her the type of service she remembered from back home.

"I don't have the widest ranging skillset," he says. "I'm basically good enough to be a professional, but here's the big secret: I'm nice."

TripAdvisor

TripAdvisor began as a travel-related search engine and was at one point owned by Expedia. According to the site's founder, the original intention was to connect the information available in travel guidebooks to individuals who were searching the web for destination and travel information.

Remember guidebooks? Before travel websites and the internet, if we wanted to get travel information for a particular city or region, we went to the library or a bookstore and picked up a guidebook that offered details on getting to and from the destination as well as information on hotels, restaurants, and attractions. TripAdvisor, and sites like it, changed how we research destinations and how we make travel decisions by offering users the ability to quickly and easily post reviews online. Interestingly, this was only a small component of the original website, but it quickly gained traction from users and then redefined the site and how many of us make travel decisions today.

TripAdvisor split off from Expedia in 2011 and is now publicly traded on NASDAQ. The company has its fingers in many different travel pots, as it has built affiliations and made acquisitions of travel and review sites around the globe. However, its core offering is user-generated content in the form of ratings, reviews, and photos—to the tune of about 350 million unique monthly visitors and 320 million reviews and opinions covering more than 6.2 million accommodations, restaurants, and attractions. TripAdvisor sites operate in 48 markets worldwide.

TripAdvisor is easily accessed through its website but also has a robust mobile app for both smartphones and tablets. Many travelers use apps and mobile phones to research travel options.

Unlike sites like Yelp, which focuses on businesses across a wide swath of industries, TripAdvisor focuses exclusively on the travel trade. Reviews break down like this:[10]

- one million bed and breakfasts and specialty lodging
- 775,000 vacation rentals
- four million restaurants
- 655,000 attractions

TripAdvisor has been a boon for many smaller businesses in the travel world. In Chapter 3, I discussed my experience with Adventure Harbor Tours in Charleston, South Carolina. It became one of the top attractions in the area by providing a great customer experience and through promotion on sites like TripAdvisor.

In conversations with TripAdvisor executives, I learned that such experiences are common. One executive told me that he has met owners of hotels and restaurants who have literally wept tears of joy when he met them in person at conferences. At the same time, some business owners feel like reviews on TripAdvisor are not reflective of the actual business. As is the case with all review sites, some folks will be unhappy.

I spoke with an executive in industry relations at TripAdvisor, and he outlined key ways that business owners can get the most from the site.

Provide Great Hospitality

Above all, reviews are driven by customers and their experiences with the hotel, restaurant, or attraction that they are patronizing. If the overall experience matches the expectations for customers, TripAdvisor says that it will be reflected in the reviews. In fact, the company says that 93 percent of surveyed users have said that their experiences largely met the expectations set by the reviews. Of course, just saying that you should provide great service doesn't provide a whole lot of guidance. Every business aspires to offer great service, particularly those in the travel arena. However, TripAdvisor can be used as a means to sniff out deficiencies in your organization's service. By keeping tabs on reviews, business owners can find areas of improvement. In fact, some reviewers will explain, often in great detail, what they liked and didn't like about their customer experience. In addition, by providing great hospitality, a business can use reviews as a tremendous equalizer. According to TripAdvisor, some hotel chains that are not traditionally known for providing great service are the top-ranked hotels in their particular markets because the management is offering great experiences and being rewarded by happy customers. This is why you may see, for example, a Super 8 outranking a Marriott in a market. Great hospitality is recognized and realized by good reviews and higher rankings.

Fresh Content Increases Page Views

Travelers want to see recent information and fresh content. Through its own surveys, TripAdvisor has learned that this validates the position of the business in the eyes of the consumer. Travelers are most interested in recent reviews and new and high quality images. If a visitor views a listing on the site and doesn't see fresh content, then they wonder why this is the case. Is the restaurant still in business? Has no one been happy since last fall, for example? According to TripAdvisor, businesses need to have great photo and video content as there's a direct correlation between high quality images and customer behavior. And TripAdvisor rewards this content, as its executives admit that brand managers who post excellent content frequently can influence engagement and affect how properties, restaurants, and attractions rank. Higher rankings get more views, and more views lead to more bookings.

Practically speaking, hotels, restaurants, rental properties, and attractions should take a hard look at their listings on TripAdvisor and realize that having an up-to-date and attractive listing on the site may be equally important as pretty brochures and a slick website.

Engagement Continues to Be Key

Sites like TripAdvisor enable the owner of a property, restaurant, or attraction the option to respond to reviewers publicly, and this has become another key aspect of managing one's reputation on the site.

First, TripAdvisor analyzed its user data and found that properties that had engaged owners who responded to reviews (both positive and negative) and posted fresh content had nearly 400 percent more page views than properties without high engagement. Management engagement may be one of the best secret weapons available to a business owner. In the early days of the site, business owners learned that some customers who had researched the property on TripAdvisor actually asked to meet the person who was responding to reviews. It offers an opportunity to actually become connected with customers on a first-name basis.

Next, engagement runs both ways. A business can thank a customer for leaving a good review and build on the relationship. In addition, it offers another opportunity to turn a negative review around and make a positive impression.

No business is perfect, and we have already learned that customers don't necessarily trust a business that has a perfect record of reviews. But a conversation (offline or online) can turn the negative into a positive.

For example, if a reviewer offers a two-star review to a hotel because he thought the bed was lumpy, an engaged owner can investigate the problem and let the reviewer know that the issue has been resolved. The response also gives the owner an opportunity to explain why the issue may have occurred or if a resolution has already been offered—such as replacing that bed. Lastly, it gives the owner a chance to tell their side of the story and even offer further information on how the beds are currently being replaced or information on another important initiative or differentiator.

Now will the two-star reviewer change his opinion? Perhaps not, but the business owner has used the opportunity to educate not only the reviewer but, more important, the next potential customer about the latest and greatest info about the property.

My family stayed in a rental home that was in a great location and very spacious, but I chose to give it four-star review because the appliances and furnishings were a bit too tired for what we paid and were expecting. In my review, I gave precise reasons why I chose four instead of five stars. My hope is that someday soon the owner of the rental house will update the kitchen and change out the lumpy sofa—and then let the community know about it. When the next potential customer comes along, he may see that new appliances are available and that news may lead to a booking.

TripAdvisor also has tools that enable big brands to track how active their managers are with engaging customers.

Dealing with Negative Reviews on TripAdvisor

While sites like TripAdvisor have many success stories, some business owners feel like they are unfairly treated and negatively impacted by low reviews. Content integrity is a top priority for the company, and the site has several hundred employees who are dedicated to this concern. From the early days of the site, the founders of TripAdvisor were concerned about the possibility of attempts to game their system.

Each property has a specific dashboard that includes resources to manage reputation issues and dispute reviews. Contingencies are set up if reviews get past the site's automated and human screens. If a business believes a review is fake or in violation of the site's guidelines, he recommends offering as much information as possible about the questionable review for TripAdvisor's dispute team to analyze.

TripAdvisor also enables a business to protest a review if it doesn't follow the site's specific guidelines. It is a family site, so reviews should be for all audiences or at least PG-13. The site is also readily on the lookout for hate speech and smear campaigns made by competitors.[11]

For example, executives note that the reviews on the site must be travel-related. If, for example, the neighbor of a bed and breakfast doesn't like the sight of a legally permitted dumpster, the neighbor can't go on TripAdvisor and write a negative review about the property. The review must relate to the travel experience and not the neighbor's opinion of the dumpster. Such a review would be successfully disputed with the site.

For those who want to dispute a review, the best course of action is to take a close look at the content of the review and analyze it against the terms and conditions. Unfortunately, your options are limited if the review is accurate and represents a bona fide customer experience. If a customer visited your restaurant on your worst of days and the service was slow and the food was cold—and you were blasted on TripAdvisor because of it—there is very little that can be done with regard to that single review.

While the negative review may be painful in the short term, TripAdvisor's algorithm will give this review less weight over time. The short term solution is to ask your existing customers for reviews, with the hope that such reviews will be positive and outweigh the negatives over time. TripAdvisor gives value to recency, as the site's executives believe that more current experiences are worth more to the site's visitors than a property's reputation from years earlier.

Here lies an important distinction between Yelp and TripAdvisor, both of which have hotel and restaurant ratings as key components on their sites. While Yelp wants reviews to be truly organic and its algorithm punishes first-time and one-time reviewers, TripAdvisor plainly encourages hotel, restaurant, and attraction owners to ask for reviews. TripAdvisor doesn't fear the so-called drive-by reviews that are in such disfavor at Yelp.

Reporting a Review on TripAdvisor

Any registered member of TripAdvisor can report a review. A small flag appears on the lower right corner of each review, and when you hover over the flag, the site asks if you want to report the review.

After choosing one of the above options, it will ask for specific information such as websites, e-mail addresses, or staff names that will help TripAdvisor's investigation. Reported reviews will be analyzed by the site and considered for deletion.

For those who want to capitalize on TripAdvisor and manage reviews, one solution is to invest in a review management system as described later in this chapter. Such systems enable a business owner who has captured e-mail addresses to solicit reviews in a systematic manner and funnel customers with positive experiences to sites like TripAdvisor. The final option is to seek out professional assistance with companies that have successfully disputed reviews.

For more information on working with TripAdvisor, visit http://www.tripadvisorsupport.com.

Case Study

TripAdvisor as a Tool to Measure Customer Satisfaction

For more than eight years, Adam Sperling has managed the Hotel Commonwealth, a top Boston hotel near the legendary Fenway Park and Boston University. As an independent hotel not flying the flag of a major chain, Sperling continually looks for ways to distinguish his high-end boutique property from its competitors. He quickly learned that TripAdvisor, now hosting more than 320 million visitors per month, provides just such a platform.

For many years, the hotel's primary source of customer feedback came from comment cards, which Sperling admits typically trickled in at a rate of about 10 per month. Sperling chose to take the comment cards out of the equation in 2010 and instead ask guests to review the hotel on TripAdvisor. Today, the Hotel Commonwealth receives 10–15 reviews per week, and it consistently ranks among the top five hotels in the market on TripAdvisor. At the time of our conversation, it was at number five but has been as high as number one. TripAdvisor reviews remain the hotel's primary means to measure customer satisfaction.

Of course, TripAdvisor engagement alone can't make a property a market leader. Sperling and his team focus intently on providing a great guest experience at the well-located and luxurious property. According to Sperling, 95 percent of the feedback is positive, and he uses the few negative comments as a training tool, as he knows that he and his staff can always make improvements. He sees the reviews as a way to receive transparent and unfiltered feedback from guests. "No hotel is perfect, so the transparency makes it powerful," he says.

All reviews receive a response, typically from the hotel's operations manager, and like most organizations, they look closely at the negatives. "We share feedback with our employees, but we don't read the reviews at our staff meeting," says Sperling. "We give high fives to individuals who are singled out on TripAdvisor, but we don't share negative reviews, and no one ever gets in trouble over negative feedback."

Sperling always wants to understand why a guest was unhappy, but he doesn't believe in pressing the panic button. "Ninety-nine percent of the negative reviews have to do with the building or something mechanical," he says.

"We sometimes get a negative review because we don't offer premium coffee makers in our rooms," he said, referencing how some hotels feature Nespresso or Keurig machines in their guest rooms. "We considered it but have chosen not to add those machines to our rooms—but we do offer one if a guest asks."

When a TripAdvisor reviewer recently complained about the coffee maker, the hotel operations manager explained in an online response that premium machines are available upon request. This ability to engage on TripAdvisor makes it possible to educate future guests of the option.

"TripAdvisor is a powerful customer service and marketing tool," he says. "It tells the story of the hotel experience through the eyes of the guests."

Glassdoor

Jobs and recruiting site Glassdoor enables employees and job seekers to rate companies and post reviews anonymously. It has more than eight million company reviews, CEO approval ratings, salary reports, interview reviews and questions, benefits reviews, office photos, videos, and other content.

Glassdoor also aggregates job listings from partner and affiliate sites, so it has a deep reservoir of information on companies, workplaces, and job openings. The site started in 2007 and has grown significantly in the job search world. It also promotes engagement between companies, employees, and applicants while also offering a useful suite of site analytics for human resources departments. It earns revenue through partnerships with employers and affiliates.

The site is a fascinating example of using community engagement and services to drive and keep traffic on its site. Although much of the review site landscape focuses on hotels and restaurants, the folks who founded Glassdoor realized that while we may spend a few weeks a year traveling and on vacation, we spend 40–50 hours every week during the rest of the year at work. Glassdoor has brought the review to the workplace.

While I learned a lot about the site from talking with its executives, one of the more interesting aspects of the site is its authority on search engines. A search for nearly any company with the word "jobs" next to it will likely find the company's Glassdoor listing on the first or second page of results. In some instances, the Glassdoor listing hits above the company site. When individuals research companies for potential employment, they are finding their way to Glassdoor, to the tune of 30 million unique users per month. What job seekers are finding on the site are more than 11 million reviews and ratings on more than 500,000 companies in over 190 countries.

Amazingly, many major companies have unclaimed profiles on Glassdoor while literally thousands of reviews, interview questions, and CEO ratings are being posted. Naturally, it would make sense to me that small businesses might not be paying attention to Glassdoor, but a cursory check of larger companies found some surprising things. One of my state's largest health systems, which is regularly lauded as one of the best workplaces in the country, is ignoring Glassdoor. FPL, the utility that provides power for me and nine million other people, has an unclaimed profile on Glassdoor.

Con Edison of New York has more than 225 reviews and its CEO has been rated more than 90 times, but the company is not engaged on Glassdoor. Add to this list the Houston Rockets, Los Angeles Dodgers, and the Seattle Seahawks. If your business has not yet engaged on Glassdoor, then you are not alone, but that's not necessarily a good thing.

And in the interest of equal time, some of the many companies that have chosen to play in the Glassdoor pool include Google, Apple, Starbucks, Goldman Sachs, Bank of America, and the Minnesota Timberwolves.

Employee reviews are at the heart of Glassdoor, and while it outwardly appears to be a site for job seekers, it also offers some interesting tools for employers. Companies that choose to engage on Glassdoor get access to some pretty cool data.

I spoke with Scott Dobroski, associate director of corporate communications at Glassdoor, and he explained that the site's employees work hard to create a balanced environment. For example, when a person registers on Glassdoor and wants to offer a review, the site takes some actions not seen by other review sites. Dobroski said that Glassdoor welcomes employees to register on the site with a valid e-mail address, which can include their corporate or work e-mail address or their personal e-mail address. He says the company is then able to verify the person is who they claim to be by signing in with a valid e-mail address or by signing in via Facebook. Though he didn't give precise details, he also said the company, in some cases, does some online cross-referencing to do its best to ensure that reviewers are who they say they are. This represents an authenticity check that is not seen on other review or complaint sites.

In a further commitment to balance, Glassdoor also requires reviewers to include both pros and cons in their assessments of companies. An employee must include the positives with the negatives in a Glassdoor review. Neither flat out bashing nor one-sided syrupy praise are allowed as the site requires balance.

The average company rating on Glassdoor is 3.2 on a 5.0 scale, so the site translates that to believe that about 71 percent of employees are satisfied with their employer. According to Glassdoor, we are, more or less, okay with our jobs. We don't singularly hate our jobs, but we aren't 99 percent happy either.

Glassdoor moderates reviews with both technological filters and a human touch. As with all such sites, reviews must meet community guidelines that block profanity, hate speech, and spamming. The site also prohibits reviewers from posting names of other employees or supervisors, as the site is not meant as a venue to pass judgment on co-workers. Top executives and high profile employees may be named, and the site has a specific process for rating CEOs. All reviews must pass the technological filters, and questionable reviews get kicked to a team of real people for evaluation. If a review is posted and another user believes that it is fake, suspicious, or questionable, it can be flagged for evaluation by the site's staff.

In general, Glassdoor will not take down a review unless it can be shown that it violates the site's guidelines. According to Dobroski, all content is treated equally, whether it is a review about a small company, a large corporation, or a paid sponsor. If it is a legitimate review, it is staying put.

Another area where Glassdoor stands out is its employer interface. In a clever move to encourage engagement, Glassdoor opens up its site analytics to employers who register on the site. It provides reporting similar to what one would find on Google Analytics but specifically aimed at the human resources community. The employer center enables users to manage reviews, receive alerts when new reviews are submitted, see how many people are researching their company, and view candidate demographics—age, level of education, years of experience, etc. Companies can also see how their employee satisfaction compares to key competitors across a number of metrics.

The site already claims to have 35 percent of the Fortune 500 as users, and that number is likely to grow. Dobroski offers the following tips for companies interacting with Glassdoor.

The Genie Is Out of the Bottle, So Sign Up

Online review sites have arrived, and the transparency they provide for users is being embraced across a wide swath of users. Companies should claim their profiles with a free employer account so that prospective employees get a truer picture of the organization and not one that is exclusively defined by Glassdoor reviews.

Build Your Profile

Job seekers are embracing employer reviews and looking for engaged companies on sites like Glassdoor. Employers should build their online profile and make sure that contact data and background information is up to date, at a minimum. Employers should also consider adding photos and detailed company information.

Encourage Employees to Write Reviews

Glassdoor wants employees to write reviews, and the site has no issues with employers who encourage employees to submit reviews. Unlike Yelp, which wants reviews to happen organically, Glassdoor believes its filters help prevent false reviews, and the site doesn't appear to be worried about ballot box stuffing. Glassdoor will provide companies with tools and templates that can be used to ask employees to post reviews, and the company has a dedicated manager whose job is to help companies engage and build out their presence on Glassdoor, which includes encouraging employees to share more reviews. Glassdoor warns against incentivizing reviews and distinguishes this from asking and encouraging. Incentivizing employees to leave reviews on Glassdoor is in direct violation of its guidelines, and Dobroski says it won't be tolerated.

Engage the Community

Like most review sites, Glassdoor encourages user engagement. Though employers are not notified of the identity of the reviewer (and Glassdoor says it will never disclose this information), the site recommends responding to both positive and negative reviews. According to the site, 62 percent of job seekers say their perception of a company improves after seeing an employer respond to a review.

Use the Free Tools

Glassdoor's employer center provides much more than engagement tools. The site's analytics provide metrics on job seekers across a wide range of data points. The tools can be used to measure against competitors or look for areas of improvement.

For more information on Glassdoor, visit *http://help.glassdoor.com*.

Angie's List

Angie's List was one of the earliest sources of consumer-driven reviews as the company predates the internet. Co-founder Angie Hicks started the business in 1995 along with her boss, venture capitalist Bill Oesterle, who at the time was having trouble finding a reliable building contractor in Columbus, Ohio. In its infancy, Hicks literally knocked on doors, soliciting consumers to sign up for the then-paid service that included a list of service providers such as plumbers, roofers, contractors, etc.

In its earliest incarnation, the business published its list in a magazine format and drew its revenues from subscriptions. Subscribers would actually call Hicks (yes, on a telephone, and maybe even a rotary one), and she would read reviews that she had received from other subscribers about the different service providers on her list. When it came time to scale the company, originally called Columbus Neighbors, they changed the name to Angie's List.

The company launched its fully interactive website in 2002 and has had significant growth since then. Today, Angie's List functions as an e-commerce marketplace with more than three million members and more than 10 million verified reviews in 720 categories, ranging from home improvement to healthcare. Hicks now serves as chief marketing officer for the company and has done well for herself since her days of knocking on doors. When Angie's List went public in 2011, her share of the company was estimated at $12 million.

The company made news recently when it dramatically altered its business model, switching away from user-paid subscriptions and opening up its membership to anyone who registers. It's believed this change was made due to increased competition from free services such as Yelp and fear that Facebook may enter the review industry with its Facebook Services offering.

Angie's List members grade companies on a report card scale from A to F. Ratings are based on price, quality, responsiveness, punctuality, and professionalism. The overall grade is an average of the grades given by customers. Unlike some other sites, Angie's List does not allow anonymous reviews. Companies wishing to advertise on the site and pay for premium positions on the site's search results must have an overall B grade or higher.

Angie's List moderates reviews in ways that are completely different from other review sites. First, if a company's overall grade is below a B, then it is not able to advertise on the site and compete for paid premium placements.

Second, if a company gets a C rating or lower, Angie's List automatically contacts the customer to inquire about the review. If there's an unresolved issue, Angie's List may, under certain circumstances, reach out to the company, explaining the complaint and a desired resolution. If the company in question does not respond or fails to follow through on a promise to resolve a customer situation, the company may be placed in Angie's List's Penalty Box.

While in the Penalty Box, a notice is placed on the company's profile, and it is excluded from category and keyword searches. In addition, it may be featured on the Penalty Box section of Angie's List's online publication. A company can escape the Penalty Box at any time by resolving the complaint.

Though the Penalty Box feels like online shaming (probably because it is), Angie's List also offers a place on its site where business owners can get extra kudos. Companies that do an extraordinary job for their clients can be nominated for the Page of Happiness. If nominated, a company may earn a special badge on its listing that says "featured on the Page of Happiness" or "Page of Happiness nominee."

Third, if a company disagrees with a review, it can petition Angie's List and ask for the review to be investigated. Angie's List will contact the user who posted the review on the company's behalf and research the complaint. If the negative review was made in error or if a dispute has been resolved, then the user can remove or modify the review.

And here's another very interesting one that business owners could learn to love. If a company and an Angie's List user are in a dispute and agree to let the website mediate it through its complaint resolution process, then the negative review may ultimately be taken down. For example, let's say a consumer hires a plumbing company from Angie's List and pays the plumber $100 to fix a leaky faucet. After a couple days, the faucet still leaks, so the consumer reaches out to the plumber who then fails to fix it. In response, the consumer gives the plumber an F grade on Angie's List. As part of its normal process, the site will reach out to the consumer and offer assistance. If certain requirements are met, then Angie's List will contact the plumber and try to remedy the issue by, for example, asking the plumber to return to the job and fix the leak or offer a refund to the consumer. If the consumer and the plumber have agreed to the complaint resolution process, then once the faucet is fixed or the customer gets their refund, then the negative F review is removed from the site.

If the consumer chooses to submit another review on the same service provider, it must be an A or a B rating, otherwise Angie's List will remove it. Using this leverage, the site helps users get better outcomes while also leveling the review playing field for businesses.

Here are some additional guidelines for success on Angie's List.

Early to Bed, Early to Rise, Work Like Hell, and Advertise

Borrowing a line from cable television mogul and highly quotable billionaire Ted Turner, the best way to have success on Angie's List is to offer good products and work hard on behalf of your customers, but you should also advertise. Angie's List offers premium placement to companies that advertise on its site, but you only get to advertise if your overall grade is B or better.

Recency Matters

On Angie's List, newer reviews carry different weight than older reviews. The "recent" column shows the average grade a company has earned over the previous three years while the "all" column lists the average that a company has received all time across all service categories. After surveying its users, the site decided that three years was a fair reflection of the company's body of work, so it makes this distinction. For companies on Angie's List, the recent column may be a blessing or a curse. Negative reviews that are older than three years won't be included in the more current ranking, but any new negative reviews may have a greater impact.

Build a Profile and Engage

Like most review sites, Angie's List also recommends that companies build out their profile pages and engage with the community as a means to increase overall traffic.

For more information on Angie's List, visit *www.angieslist.com/faq*.

Review Software Can Drive Positive Feedback

All companies want positive reviews, but some business owners are hesitant to ask for them because they fear that they are inviting negative feedback. It's a common fear despite the fact that the majority of online reviews are positive. Business owners and CEOs have told me that even though they believe in the concept of transparency, they still fear that engagement on review sites will lead to negative overall ratings. I truly understand this as I have had the same thoughts about my business, but in the end, it is a bit of an irrational fear. Just as I tell visitors to Florida that they are more likely to be struck by lightning or hit by an asteroid than being attacked by a shark, it doesn't make them any less afraid of the water.

So we have a conundrum. We want positive reviews, but we are afraid of the negative ones (and we will never watch the movie *Jaws* again). A number of smart computer programmers have figured out a solution that has taken on the name of review management software. Here's how it works.

First, a company must secure e-mail addresses from its customers as the software is completely based on outreach through e-mail. Customer e-mail addresses will need to be loaded into the review management software system—which will more than likely be cloud-based and completely managed online. If you are billing customers via e-mail or clients are contacting you online, then you may already have client e-mail addresses. If not, you need to develop a system to capture this data by, for example, offering an incentive for them to join an e-mail mailing list or by asking them to take a survey. Ultimately, you will be surveying them, so this tactic might be the best bet.

Second, the software will send a short e-mail survey to your clients, asking them to rate their customer experience and to leave a comment. For example, a hotel owner may ask the customer to rate their stay on a scale of 1–10. Or a retailer may ask if the store met all of their expectations and rate it on the same scale.

Lastly, the results of the short survey dictate what happens next. If the customer gives a 10 out of 10 score, then the software can be configured to immediately send a follow-up message, asking that the customer visit a review site of your choosing (Google, Yelp, TripAdvisor, Angie's List, or practically any other) and leave a review of your company. You may decide to only funnel scores of 9 or above in this way.

For lower scores, the software will notify the business owner that a customer was not completely satisfied, giving the business an opportunity to reach out to that customer and find out if they need additional attention. And if it is a particularly low rating, this notification may give the business a needed heads-up to a customer who might be unhappy enough to leave a negative review elsewhere. Remember, you are only steering the happy customers to TripAdvisor, for example. The unhappy ones aren't redirected, but instead the business is given a chance to turn them around.

Review management software has some pros and cons. On the positive side, it offers a systemized approach to help secure reviews. Once you set up the system and input your client e-mail addresses, the software does the rest. The business owner can focus on addressing any negative feedback while, hopefully, watching positive reviews roll in. It can be a powerful customer satisfaction tool.

On the con side of the equation, sending customers e-mail through a third-party service may cause privacy issues for some businesses, such as those in financial services or healthcare. In addition, asking for reviews in this manner defies best practices for sites like Yelp, and using such a system may not generate recommended ratings on Yelp as reviews generated through this process might be easily flagged by the site's algorithm as drive-bys. Also, review management software doesn't provide a quick fix. In my experience, a fairly small percentage of customers who are asked to visit a review site actually follow through. So you may need to funnel hundreds of customers in order to secure a handful of positive reviews.

On the whole, review management software offers a solid, systemized approach to promote positive reviews and is worth investigating if you have concerns about negative feedback on the main bona fide review sites.

Chapter 5:
Build Your Reputation with Ongoing Marketing Activities

One of the best ways to protect your online reputation over the long haul is by increasing your existing online marketing efforts. By building your online profile with activities like blogging, applying for awards, and telling authentic stories distributed through strong marketing challenges, you can create your online firewall while also improving your sales and marketing activities.

One thing that I often hear from executives is that they want to improve their corporate communications, marketing, and public relations, but they don't know where to start. Perhaps the conversation begins with an executive saying they want a presence on social media, they want to blog, or they just want to "get their name out there." How do you do it? How do you develop a communications strategy? The answer is to get your GAME on.

Communications Strategy 101: Get your GAME on

While developing a complete communications strategy takes research and in-depth planning, one can make the first moves fairly easily and can quickly point the ship in the right direction. This process, which can take a few hours for a cursory approach or several weeks for a deep dive, focuses on four areas: Goals, Audiences, Messaging (and tactics), and Evaluation. GAME. Get it? (Don't feel the need to be snarky about the *t* in "tactics." It's my process, so I'm calling it GAME.)

Goals

To paraphrase one of the greatest vice-presidential debate quotes of all time from Admiral Stockdale in 1992, "who are we, and why are we here?"

What are your communications goals? The answer to this may seem simple, as it almost always points to sales growth, but let's be more specific. Is your business new and unknown (or just quiet marketing-wise), and would you like to use communications to build name recognition? Are you well-known in the marketplace but have changed your product or service, so you need to educate an existing audience? Do you need to reach potential partners? Do you have a perfect handle on your marketing goals and need to flood the market with your message? Are there multiple related goals?

Take the time to identify your main communications goals. Hone in on and identify clean, measurable goals.

Audiences

Dollar for dollar, this is the most important aspect of a communications strategy, in my humble opinion. I have done the GAME exercise with dozens of companies, and almost every time, we come away with renewed focus on an under-served audience.

For the sake of brevity, let's look at a typical goal: A company wants to use communications to generate leads. Sounds easy enough, right?

Well, not so fast. We need to answer some key questions about the audience. I like to start with current customers to identify the channels that turn prospects into clients. Who are these customers, and where did they come from? Did most of them come from advertising? Are most clients acquired from referral sources? Do you get your business from brokers of one kind or another? Take a hard look, and get specific about who your customers are and where they come from. (If a business owner tells me that anyone can be their client, I'm usually eyeing the exit.)

Perhaps at the moment, many new clients come through some form of broker relationship. This can be clear in a business that receives real estate or insurance work from an established broker relationship. Or this relationship could include a law firm that receives referrals from other lawyers, who are paid a referral fee. Such relationships are often critical to businesses of all sorts, but they aren't necessarily the most profitable—because you have to pay the referral fee, commission, or consulting fee. In many cases, businesses want to improve their communications with the end-user—and acquire customers directly, without a broker.

So the end-user is one key audience, but you may also find that other trusted advisors to this audience may be in a position to make referrals without requiring commissions. I have seen this occur many times. Dig in as much as possible, and find those profitable audiences. Make sure you understand what motivates them and how they make decisions that impact your business. You can't know too much about these audiences.

Messaging (and tactics)

So you have your goals, and you are getting intimate with your audience. What are you going to say, and how will you reach that audience?

Here's where you get to make your pitch. What makes your company, firm, or product a better fit for your audience? What's the elevator speech for this audience? What problem does your offering solve that your competitors' products don't? Is this the time to pound away on better customer service?

For each audience that you have segmented, develop three to five main message points for each. These may cover unique product attributes, expertise, pricing, or service—or some combination of these. Again, take some time and focus.

Next, review the multitudes of communications strategies available to reach your audience with your key messages. For example:

- speaking opportunities at industry conferences or association meetings
- e-mail marketing
- article placements in industry publications
- direct mail
- advertising on industry websites or e-mail newsletters and retargeting ads
- a blog that promotes your messaging in an interesting and informative way

Evaluation

Once you have your messaging and your tactics down, how will you evaluate the program? What does success look like 12 months from now for a communications program?

In the public relations business, this is often the Holy Grail: measurement. My recommendation is that you set realistic expectations and moderate goals. Look for ways to measure the cost of leads compared to other programs. Review the value of media placements and how you can repackage them as parts of marketing materials.

Remember to ask your clients and prospects how they heard about you and how they felt about the messaging. Track web traffic from e-blasts, blog posts, and social media mentions. Compare this to other traffic, and determine overall effectiveness.

And don't underestimate intangibles. The credibility boost from media placements is a real thing, for example, though hard to put a price tag on.

Once you have your strategy set, pull together the right team to execute it.

Storytelling Returns to Marketing

What do every great movie, book, and marketing campaign have in common? The answer is: a great story. Now this may seem like an old mantra, but as internet marketing dominated our agendas in recent years, we focused our energy heavily (and a bit too much in my opinion) on keywords, tags, short-form posts, tweets, etc. While it's okay to be brief in your communications, we can't let our story suffer because of the medium. And with the continued fragmentation of media, we need to return to telling stories because it sets our message apart and helps our meaning ring clear amid the noise in the marketplace of attention.

Part of the beauty of the internet is that it democratized marketing. Anyone can write a blog that is easily searchable and findable. We can make our own videos, which can go viral and reach millions of eyeballs. The internet is the world's biggest open-for-business sign and has profoundly changed how we market.

But as the web has found its way as a tool, it has also influenced how we communicate. For a period of time, to build awareness we were blasting out as much information as we could—and the story suffered. Every search engine optimization company would write "press releases" that said virtually nothing and distribute them to "article farm" websites that published them. No story, no message, just keywords and gobbledygook, which somehow improved search results. The smart folks at Google figured it out and have since implemented ongoing changes that favor—yep, you guessed it—original, meaningful content.

We need to return to telling our stories and engaging our audience with interesting information. The good news is that rather than being forced to develop thousands of pieces of nutrition-free content, you can be smarter about what you're distributing.

I have been noodling over this topic for a while, but a couple of pieces of communications caught my attention that are prime examples of the power of storytelling. The first was LeBron James's "essay" in *Sports Illustrated* announcing his departure from the Miami Heat.[1] I found it to be a strong piece of public relations communications that explained James's position in a way that was believable and authentic.

The second was an exceptional article written by Chip Bergh, CEO of Levi Strauss & Co., who generated a ton of buzz back in May of 2014 when he suggested that you should never wash your jeans.[2] The story was picked up by news outlets across the country, including *Good Morning America*. While the buzz had little depth, the published response told a real story.

In an essay that first appeared on LinkedIn as "The Dirty Jeans Manifesto," Bergh went into detail about how jeans ought to be washed infrequently, by hand, in cold water, and dried on a line, but he also seized the opportunity to talk about sustainability. Now, jeans that are never washed and last for years meet a lot of my sustainability tests, but Bergh also explained how Levi's has dug deep into this issue. Because it was part of a compelling story, I listened. Here's a little bit of it:

"An average pair of jeans consumes roughly 3,500 liters of water—and that is after only two years of use, washing the jeans once a week. Nearly half of the total water consumption, or 1,600 liters, is the consumer throwing the jeans in the washing machine. That's equivalent to 6,700 glasses of drinking water!"

The piece went on to explain what Levi's had done to reduce water consumption in its manufacturing process and also how the company offered guidance to consumers on how to reduce their carbon footprint by washing jeans the way Bergh professed. He said he washed them himself and that his wife could attest to that fact.

By weaving the sustainability message into the story about how often one should wash your jeans, Bergh made a lot of people aware of the company's positioning. Before reading the story, I had never thought for a second about the sustainability of my favorite skinny jeans, but it's now on my radar—though I don't think I have ever worn any brand other than Levi's.

Bergh posted his "manifesto" on LinkedIn, and it was later published on the *Huffington Post*. The story drove it to wider circulation.

Of course, writing something compelling and posting it on LinkedIn doesn't guarantee it will get viral legs, but that's where professional communications comes into play. We need to look at all options, paid and otherwise, to get our stories in front of larger audiences.

Changing the Public Relations Channel

As I have told my stunned teenage children, when I was a kid we only had four television channels. Back in the day (and by this I mean before anyone ever said "back in the day"), before cable television, before the internet, and way before a full season of *House of Cards* dropped in one day, we had four televison options: the local affiliate stations for ABC, CBS, NBC, and PBS. Television channels were broadcast over the airwaves (not Wi-Fi), and some televisions only showed footage in black and white. Our viewing choices and channels were very limited, but we didn't know any better. Oh yeah, there was an informal fifth channel that I will call the shut-off-the-television-and-go-play-outside channel, but the details of that one are best left to another day.

I have been thinking about communications and distribution channels for our marketing messages. We need to seek them out, manage them, sometimes pay for them, and often create our own. We also need to develop our distribution channels so our story can be widely consumed by our target audience.

Find a partner. In the public relations business back in the day (there it is again), we would write press releases and distribute them to reporters at dailies, weeklies, and those four television stations. We used (cue gasp) snail mail, and later faxes, and then e-mail. Our so-called partners were media outlets and reporters and editors who worked for them. We wanted our partners to write or broadcast stories about our clients. But as the media industry has become more fragmented and news staffs thinner, partner relationships are much harder to come by.

But all is not lost. These outlets, and many new ones, still want our information, but we have to package it differently. We have more opportunities than ever to write articles and posts for bona fide news outlets. For example, I have secured blogging slots for clients on sites like the *Huffington Post* and *Forbes*. But we also have trade outlets in many industries thirsting for good content. Many are willing to publish your stories; you just have to seek them out. Sometimes it's as simple as asking.

Bite the bullet and pay for it. The traditional bailiwick of the public relations pro is publicity and media coverage that one doesn't pay for. The current term of art is "earned media." However, many media outlets offer distribution channels that are not traditional public relations opportunities (meaning not free), but they aren't traditional advertising either, though they do have a price tag. For example, *Forbes* has a section called BrandVoice, which integrates marketers' content with *Forbes*'s editorial and users' content. If you sign up and pay its fees, it will give your story prominence on its website. Companies like IBM and SAP currently run case studies and other stories that appear in the news and search streams but are not editorial content written by a *Forbes* reporter or contributor. *Forbes* can help drive people to your story, but in this case, for a price. While I might have shrugged off such an offering as "pay for play" when I first started in the public relations business, today I can't. It's a viable way to get your story told, even if it might feel more like advertising and less like publicity.

Other services, flying under the banner of content marketing, enable you to pay to place your blog posts on top websites like CNN.com, NBCNews.com, and Marketwatch.com (run by The *Wall Street Journal*). It won't run in the news stream but will appear in sections, usually at the bottom of the page, titled "Content from Our Sponsors" or "Around the Web." These are typically pay-per-click sections, and a number of online companies can set you up on them rather quickly.

Develop your own channel. If you can't find a good partner arrangement and you don't want to pay for content marketing, you can create your own channel. Many businesses have had the makings of their own channel for years. It probably started with the holiday card list, which has since morphed into the e-mail blast list. Add in all those contacts buried in your Outlook and you have the beginnings of your own channel. Combine this with your LinkedIn contacts and your Twitter and Facebook followers, and you'll start to get some traction and reach. E-mail blast providers can help you set up a distribution system in short order. And you can consider augmenting this with a purchased or borrowed list. Beware the spam rules, and your own channel can be up and running in no time.

As the media business shifts, we have to also consider changing the public relations channel. It takes some effort, but any business can develop a distribution system that offers great benefit.

The Race Back to Actual News

Way back in the late 1990s, I began telling people that the internet might kill newspapers but that it wouldn't end journalism. A robust free press remains part of the fabric of our nation, even as we continue to struggle with how to pay for it. Remember, journalism was created to educate, inform, and persuade people, and our nation's first journalists were not writing to please advertisers. Thomas Paine did not write *Common Sense* as a vehicle to promote furniture discounts, closeout sales, or classifieds. Advertising was a by-product of journalism, which has, at times, overshadowed it—but I promise you, journalism will endure.

The late *New York Times* reporter David Carr, who covered the media business (and did it very well, by the way), wrote an interesting piece in 2014 that got me thinking. He noted that the *Washington Post* under new ownership of Jeff Bezos had flourished recently because it bolstered its newsroom after years of staff cuts. The *Washington Post* had begun turning out more scoops and generating traction. It's not clear how that affected the balance sheet, but the newsroom became healthier than it had been for some time. In 2012, Carr wrote, presciently, that actual news was likely the next "killer app." It was not just the *Washington Post*; other outlets were looking at real news instead of the puffery that had dominated our social streams.

When the internet came along and turned the media business on its ear, we watched as print outlets slowly evolved into media companies trying to figure out how to structure their new web-based editions. Do we charge for it? Part of it? Do we give it away?

In the interim, alternative sites popped up, and some drew immense amounts of traffic. The *Huffington Post* has more visitors than CNN, The *New York Times,* or the *Wall Street Journal.* Sites such as Buzzfeed and Mashable have more traffic than, or at least comparable to, the old-school dailies such as the *Dallas Morning News* and the *Miami Herald.*

What's new is that these sites—having made most of their living on social shares, content curation, and listicles (those five-top-this and 10-best-that stories)—are now getting heavily into the actual news business, as mentioned by Carr. Mashable's executive editor was formerly with Reuters and the *Times*; Buzzfeed's editor-in-chief came over from Politico. If you follow Buzzfeed's founder Jonah Peretti on Twitter, you'll notice that he regularly pumps up the website's original reporting, investigations, and scoops. He doesn't trumpet the other top content that currently makes him a lot of money, such as these listicles: "17 Reasons It's Way Better to Date a Dog Person" and "60 Ridiculously Pretty Nail Art Designs You'll Want to Copy Immediately."

What these sites have done is to hire real journalists because actual news has originality, relevance, and authenticity. They want content that no one else has, that's new, and that has a bit of "unknowness" (that might not be a word), because this type of information has a better chance of driving traffic and virility.

What does this mean for businesses? The answer is the point I have been hammering away at for a while. We need to create new, interesting, and authentic communications for our audiences. We can't just slap our name on the news of the day and call it a blog, and we can't just slap our twist on someone else's work and expect it to make us stand out. (As mentioned earlier, Google figured that out and it doesn't work.) We have to develop meaningful messaging for our audiences.

What should we do next? Go take a look at the smartest guys in the room. Bezos is artfully doing it at the *Washington Post.* Peretti, who practically invented social sharing, is doing it at Buzzfeed. They are focusing on news and meaningful, authentic communications.

Social Sharing Feeds Our Appetite for News

A few years ago, when traveling to meet a client, a story about his business was published in the local newspaper that very morning. Because we had placed the story, I proudly asked my client if he had seen the morning paper. He handed me a faxed copy of the article—not an original. I was taken aback.

"You don't get your local paper?" I asked.

"Haven't for a while," he replied.

"How do you get your news?" I queried.

"Well, I get The *Wall Street Journal* at my house, but I dropped the local paper a while ago," he said. "If it's important, someone will send it to me."

This happened in 2009 and should have been a clear signal to divest immediately all print media company holdings.

I bring up this story not to discuss the long-studied decline of printed dailies but, rather, the latter part of the statement: "If it's important, someone will send it to me." Back in 2009, faxing an article was equivalent to today's social media sharing. If you have ever posted a news link to Facebook, Twitter, or Instagram, then you have participated in the social sharing ecosystem that is overtaking traditional channels as the most powerful way to distribute information.

Reporter Claire Cain Miller in The *New York Times* wrote that rising news website Buzzfeed now gets more traffic from Facebook than from Google.[3] Popular thinking was that search engines drove the most traffic to news sites, but a shift is on. The following is from Miller's article: "In 2013, 40 percent of traffic came from search engines, and 14 percent came from social networks. In 2014, about 29 percent of traffic comes from each."

This, of course, begs the question, how do you get your news? We know that fewer and fewer folks get a daily printed paper, but we remain informed (I hope), so people still get information somehow.

Is it through search engines, frequent visits to news websites, or, as Miller suggests, social sharing? Likely, it's an evolving combination.

I decided to ask a few executive-level friends how they got their news. My sample skewed "old school," but that's part of my point.

One exec read a national newspaper online each day and got a hard copy on the weekends. He also relied on Twitter for breaking news and Google Alerts for specific topics, as well as trade outlet news briefs for the latest news in his particular industry. He read articles funneled through social media but didn't conscientiously share news on a regular basis.

Another exec eschewed social media completely, claiming that his Facebook account was "stillborn" (that cracked me up). His morning ritual included The *New York Times* on his tablet, along with a glance at his local daily online. He also read other online publications and shared content regularly—but via e-mail, not social media. No e-mail news alerts, as he found them intrusive.

I posed the same question to a small business owner. He replied that he hadn't read a newspaper in years. He had hit some hard times during the Great Recession and said that all the bad news in the paper, on television, and on the radio depressed him, so he dropped his subscriptions and only listened to satellite radio in his car. Business had recovered, by the way, but he still didn't subscribe to a paper.

I asked all three one simple question: "How did you learn of the death of Robin Williams?" In August 2014 it was a big news story, and most people remember how they heard about it. The first exec said via Twitter, the second said from the CNN website, and the third (who said he didn't follow the news at all) answered Facebook—which was a bit of a light bulb moment for both of us.

I agree with *New York Times* reporter Miller's findings that social sharing is gaining ground. Many folks are spending more time on Facebook, Instagram, LinkedIn, and Twitter than any one news site. When news breaks, it also breaks on social media sites, and that's when we might gravitate back to traditional media outlets such as television and the big news websites. If you're like me, when you hear about major news such as military actions or the passing of a beloved entertainer, you're driven to national outlets like CNN or Fox. If we can get our general news fix via social media, though, there's very little reason to leave the comfort of our insulated feed. The social sharing ecosystem offers many of us enough information to satiate our appetite for news.

If You Think Your Audience Is an Algorithm, You're Doing it Wrong

One of the first things I learned in journalism school, and later honed in my public relations career, was the concept of knowing one's audience. For example, when writing for the general newspaper-reading public, you need to make sure your text is crafted at no more than an 11th-grade reading level. And while writing an article in a journalism class, if you throw in a bunch of heavy-duty words, you'll get crucified by the professor. In the business world, if you don't understand your audience, you can develop marketing material that goes over your audience's collective head or, worse, insults them. Remember, your audience comprises people whom you want to educate, connect with, and persuade.

Yet as communicators, in recent years we have drifted. Our emphasis has shifted away from people and instead focuses on the computer algorithms created by search engines. We write website copy overburdened with search terms, and we worry more about keyword density than meaning and message. We write copy of a length and depth that we think pleases Google rather than what our readers want. And we endure seemingly endless meetings trying to divine what terms prospects will plug into search boxes, in addition to spending millions of dollars trying to drive people to our sites. This has evolved into a problem.

Believe me, we are all in the same boat. I still cringe when I think about the keyword-dense copy I had on my site until fairly recently: "As a Miami public relations firm meeting the needs of Miami businesses with a Miami public relations solution . . ." Gag me! What the hell was I thinking? Well, I wasn't writing for people; I was writing for an algorithm at the behest of a search engine optimization expert. (In retrospect, it's even worse, because I consider myself a professional communicator. That copy was crap.)

As I have said many times, the folks at Google are way smarter than us, and the Google mission is to direct people to the information they are seeking. They have figured out that people want what they want and do not want to be driven somewhere irrelevant.

From a communications and marketing standpoint, this means it's time to move on. We need to give up trying to outsmart Google and start writing and presenting meaningful content to our audience, which, remember, is made up of people, not computers. Meaningful content will get found, be appreciated, and ultimately further your business mission.

Google knows this too, and it is leading the charge. Continuous updates to its search process have sent many companies scrambling to replace web traffic. The old tricks aren't working, and all roads are pointing to brand-building and authentic communications.

I'm not saying that publishing good content eliminates the need for search engine optimization. That craft still exists, and you still need search engine optimization-friendly content. All those meta tags and descriptions are not for naught; they're just less important than you thought. And for companies that have a mass-market audience, I highly recommend consulting with experts who are regularly analyzing the ins and outs of search, the Google algorithm updates, and the finer points of search engine optimization. But if you're in a small niche business, then you'd better be thinking about authentic, interesting, and worthwhile content and forgetting about teaching to the algorithm test.

It's important to note that I'm not just talking about search engine optimization and being found online. Storytelling and compelling visuals, as well as attention-getting video, all need to be considered as we weave our marketing tales. We can never forget that our audience is made up of people—sometimes smart, oftentimes fallible, and frequently unpredictable, but people nonetheless. They are the ones who click, who make stories go viral, and who ultimately reach into their wallets and make purchases. An algorithm will never be your customer, so don't make it your audience.

Five Reasons to Start a CEO Blog

Publish or perish! We hear about it in the context of academia all the time. In order for would-be professors to be considered for tenured positions, they need to regularly showcase their brilliance through publishing relevant scholarly works.

I would argue that CEOs should follow the same advice, though they need not regularly publish doctoral-thesis-worthy communications but rather compelling blog content that can advance their business and personal interests. Below are five reasons why companies should embrace the CEO blog.

A CEO blog can . . .

Put a face to your organization. A CEO is almost always the best single human asset that a company has, particularly in start-ups and smaller companies. Yet many businesses hide their top asset behind a marketing curtain. A perfunctory website bio, usually without contact information, makes a CEO appear inaccessible.

If your goal is to be a customer-facing and customer-focused organization, a CEO blog can create a public face for a company. Showcasing your company's personality can go a long way to defining your values.

Explain your vision to multiple audiences. A CEO blog opens communications with audiences both internal and external, offering an unfettered channel to deliver clear messaging. Every CEO has a variety of audiences, and depending on the situation and the current business goals, some may be more critical than others. A blog can be used to explain the company's latest plans for employees or show off accomplishments for potential partners or investors. The clear, unobstructed communications channel is a powerful tool.

Cue you up for thought leadership. All CEOs have a vision for their company, but they don't always have a platform to articulate that vision. In most situations, CEOs want to differentiate their company from their competitors and explain that their approach to business is industry-leading. Companies that wish to position their top executives and management team as thought leaders are missing an opportunity if they aren't using the CEO blog as a tool. When written well, a CEO blog with broad appeal can be picked up for publication in an industry media outlet or consumer channel. This may not lead to thought leadership right out of the gate, but showing a track record of solid writing and messaging helps pave the way for invitations to contribute content to thought-leading outlets. We have helped clients post hundreds of articles in trade publications as well as secured opportunities to regularly contribute to outlets like *Forbes* and the *Huffington Post*. These outlets remain selective and your content must have value, but CEOs often offer the kind of insight these outlets seek.

Build a reliable communications channel. Every CEO believes that they should be regularly communicating with key audiences, but many fail to practice it. A CEO blog can create an excellent communications channel that audience members both respect and enjoy. Creating an authentic channel can also pay off down the road if the company must explain unpleasant news such as lower revenues or something worse during a crisis. In such situations, it's best if the first communication from the CEO isn't just when the news is bad. It may seem counterintuitive, but a regular channel of authentic communications, even if it is typically good news, can be helpful in times of crisis.

Position the CEO's personal brand. Let's be real here. Every CEO will say that a blog needs to promote their *business* goals, but an ancillary benefit is that it promotes the CEO's personal brand too. Many CEOs are looking for ways to differentiate themselves and make the leap to super stardom. A CEO blog can help elevate an executive to the next level, which may lead to the next great assignment or challenge. Of course, a blog won't make any CEO dramatically better at their job, but it may help showcase an executive as a leader and an up-and-comer. Any CEO who isn't promoting their personal brand is skipping the trappings of the digital marketing age. You either want your audience to know you're a star or you don't. My guess is the former.

For CEOs wishing to get started, I recommend establishing an overall strategy, schedule, and rough editorial calendar. A CEO blog is most effective when it is part of your corporate website, but many ancillary channels currently exist to push your content out. It may seem like a daunting task, but the CEO blog challenge can be overcome with planning and some editorial insight.

Cracking the Code on Wikipedia

One of the internet's most popular websites is the free online encyclopedia called Wikipedia. The site is viewed as an objective source of information and contains entries and listings on the world's most common subjects as well as mundane and little-known topics.

Wikipedia is a classic web-based creation. While the internet itself killed the old trusty home library of encyclopedias (we had the *World Book* at my house), it was Wikipedia that drove the nails in the coffin and tossed the first handful of dirt.

After typing a general topic into any search engine, you will likely find the Wikipedia listing on the first page of search results and usually near the top. Search engines love Wikipedia because the site is oft-visited and it remains a free, self-governed site that has no advertising, shareholders, or marketing agenda.

For individuals and companies that have a listing on Wikipedia, that page will likely be the first thing that most people view when they search for you on Google. This can be a powerful marketing tool—assuming the information on the site is to your liking.

You might think, "Hey, anyone can edit it, so I will just write whatever I want!" This is true, but only to a point.

What's most fascinating about Wikipedia is that literally anyone can edit it and make entries. So, if you happen to be an expert on samurai swords, you can post information on the site about their history, manufacturing, etc. Even if you don't know a damn thing about the sharp implements, you can also post information. But beware the Wikipedia editors. They read every entry and will slice, dice, and delete you if you publish inaccurate, self-serving, or improperly attributed information.

Okay, so you think you or your company should be included in Wikipedia.

Question 1: Are you notable enough?

In my opinion, a Wikipedia listing is a badge of honor for a CEO or top executive. Many public relations people have tried and failed to get such a listing approved and published about one of their clients. Every person can't have a Wikipedia page or article—only those who are "notable."

Here's an excerpt from Wikipedia's definition of "notability:"[4]

"Article and list topics must be notable, or 'worthy of notice'. Determining notability does not necessarily depend on things such as fame, importance, or popularity—although those may enhance the acceptability of a subject . . ."

Wikipedia's community of editors reviews every listing to ensure it passes notability standards. Did the person or company mentioned create something new and different? Is the person a captain of industry? Is it a truly leading, groundbreaking company? Did he, she, or it marry a Kardashian? If you aren't notable, your proposed Wikipedia entry will not see the light of day.

Question 2: So you're notable, but can you prove it?

Remembering that Wikipedia is an internet creation, to prove you are notable, *someone else* on the internet needs to back it up. Articles published online in mainstream media outlets are the best evidence to prove notability. If the *Wall Street Journal* or The *New York Times* say you are notable, and the story is readily available online, then you have a much better chance of passing the test. If a lesser known publication wrote about you pre-internet, it is much tougher. Also, Wikipedia notability police don't care about press releases written about you, information posted about you on your website (even if it is accurate), or articles you have written for trade publications. You aren't notable unless a *third party*—like an established daily newspaper—says it, and it is easily found/linkable online.

Question 3: Can you get past, withstand, and outmaneuver the Wikipedia police?

Okay, so you believe your entry passes the notability test and you want to publish it. There are many obstacles. First, you can't publish your own entry, or the Wikipedia police will scotch it. They want entries written and posted by objective writers. Worse yet are public relations people. We in the public relations biz identified the value of Wikipedia several years ago, and the Wikipedia editors quickly decided that public relations people can't be objective. If you publish an entry and your e-mail address is [insert name]@DavidPR.com, for example, they will identify you as a public relations person and stone you. Yes, this has happened to me.

Also, even if you are the best source of information on a topic, the Wikipedia police will pounce. Years ago, we had a client that didn't like their Wikipedia entry. Silly me, I logged on to the Wikipedia page, made edits, and then noted that I was a public relations person for the client. I also noted that I would be regularly contributing to the page. Not so fast, my friend! Wikipedia editors quickly reversed all of my edits and chastised me for suggesting that anyone so close to the topic could be objective. Undaunted, I changed the edits back and thumbed my nose at the editors. My edits were again reverted, and the chastising continued. As the conversation degraded, I retreated to ponder a new approach.

If there's one thing that Wikipedia editors hate, it's someone posting an entry that in any way seems *self-serving*. So if you think you can post an article about you or your business in order to elevate your profile, forget it.

Ever been called a "sockpuppet"? A marketing person for my client, not as circumspect as me, went back and made the same edits. The Wikipedia editors decided that my client must have been me, just using another ISP. I was branded a sockpuppet—a person who impersonates another online. After a moment of being aghast, I laughed my head off.

Here's a secret. The next time I wanted to create a Wikipedia entry, I worked with a third-party editor to draft the page and completely distanced my connection (and my public-relations-guy DNA) from Wikipedia. The page topic passed the notability test, the text was properly written and attributed, and the page was eventually published. To get a page published, you have to pass all the tests and then artfully game the system so your "perceived lack of objectivity" will not be immediately noticeable to Wikipedia editors. It's tricky but not impossible. While I don't claim to be a Wikipedia expert, I do believe I have shed the sockpuppet label.

Write the Book on It

Writing a business book offers many marketing opportunities: It adds credibility, increases the author's chances to be a media source, and creates a marketing platform. If you add in that publishing your own book has never been easier and that we typically hold authors in high regard, it clearly makes sense to be the one who wrote the book on a topic. Right now, I know several executives who are either writing or have finished books on subjects as diverse as small business loans, branding, IRAs, cruise line safety, and financial planning.

While there are millions of books on the market, it's possible that you can own your niche category. For example, my friend and client Chris Hurn of Fountainhead Commercial Capital wrote his book *The Entrepreneur's Secret to Creating Wealth* about a little-known U.S. Small Business Administration loan program that helps small business owners grow their wealth by owning, rather than renting, their commercial property. Hurn was already regarded as a media source on Small Business Administration 504 loans, but publishing the book cemented him as the leading expert. He also has effectively boxed out his competitors, who may have thought about writing a book but are now likely discouraged.

Friend and branding expert Bruce Turkel has written three books, the most recent is *All About Them: Grow Your Business by Focusing on Others*. When I asked him about the benefit of writing his books, one of his first answers was credibility. "They're the best business cards ever designed, as they provide almost instantaneous credibility," he said. Turkel has spoken about branding around the world and has been a guest on a number of cable news shows. Being an author is another valuable line on his resume.

Another client is working on a book for the reasons mentioned above but also because it will help differentiate him from his competitors. If you're competing in a market with an 800-pound gorilla, then writing the book offers a way to be viewed as an expert despite the oversized bulk of your competitor. I recently advised a young entrepreneur to consider writing a book about her nascent industry. While her market isn't crowded, one major competitor secures a big share of the publicity. If the new kid on the block can write the book, then she has a credential that can be used to differentiate her company from the more established competitor.

For Hurn, his book was the cornerstone of his company's marketing for more than a year. He has done a number of local and national television appearances since his book was published as well as dozens of radio interviews to go along with blog mentions and other press coverage. Hurn talks not only about his book but also the commercial real estate market, and his company gets a favorable mention too. And for his public relations team, the credential of being an author adds to the strength of media pitches.

Upon further discussion with Turkel, I learned of yet another benefit. Your book can educate your prospects and directly aid your sales process. "If our clients or potential clients read the books and use our nomenclature when they're discussing branding, it makes it much easier for them to understand what we're talking about and to hire us," said Turkel. Just imagine the value of a prospect already speaking your language before you even start your sales pitch.

While the actual act of writing a book hasn't gotten any easier, getting published certainly has. I call it "Amazon democracy." A quick search online will find dozens of book publishers that can not only help you write your book but also secure distribution through Amazon and other online booksellers. Getting into brick-and-mortar bookstores still remains a challenge, but sadly those companies have their own issues to contend with.

Apply for Business Awards

At some point in the recent past, it became popular to include one's awards and accolades in your e-mail signature. It's now common to finish reading an e-mail and then notice that the sender's company is a "Great Place to Work" or a member of the "[insert trade magazine here] Top 100." While I don't like to see e-mail monikers overwhelmed by such plaudits, I must admit that I'm a fan of awards. I think they make good business sense for a number of reasons.

Awards and other recognition offer a compliment that sounds much better when someone else says it. Company awards also can help boost morale as they offer recognition for employees and their efforts. Awards also hearten owners, investors, and other interested parties. Further, prospective clients and future employees are often more likely to consider a company that is viewed as being one of the top in its field. Once you have won the award, make sure you promote it on your website, through your social media channels, and with a news release. It's not bragging if someone else says it. Third party validation carries weight in business. Sure, you can announce how amazing your company is, but when a third party says it, your credibility gets a bigger bump.

It also makes your clients and partners look good. In some industries (public relations for one), the best awards are for work you do on behalf of your clients. Ad agencies are another prime example. If the agency for Anheuser Busch wins an award for a campaign, the brewer gets credit too. If your company does an award-worthy job for one of its clients, then you can bet the client will be happy to also get a trophy. In my experience, aside from getting joy from calling a client and telling them that we won an award for the work we did on their behalf, it also helps bolster the relationship because most award-winning efforts build camaraderie between client and contractor, agency, or vendor. An award earned on behalf of a client also validates the quality of the work.

Awards prove that you are, in fact, "best of [blank]." Companies spend a great deal of time and energy to position their products and offerings in the best possible light. However, repeatedly saying that your stuff is the best—state-of-the-art this and best-of-breed that—is much weaker than if your company or product is specifically lauded by others as being the best. In a time when everyone is saying they are the best, awards and recognition from others can help a company distinguish itself. This is particularly valuable for businesses that offer less tangible services.

Awards also can be used to help solve business and communications challenges. For example, while consulting with a company that was struggling to find high-quality job applicants, we helped them apply to become a Best Place to Work as awarded by *Fortune*.

We also have recommended that attorneys work to secure awards and recognition. Lawyers often have difficulty distinguishing themselves from competitors because they are selling an intangible service. Being recognized as one of the top lawyers in their geographic area can be a tremendous asset.

If you are interested in applying for awards for your company, my recommendation is to start by researching local business and trade publications. For example, *American City Business Journals* has 40 publications in markets throughout the country, and most have geographic and industry-specific awards and listing programs. Also, many trade publications sponsor award programs, so it is likely that the "bible" of your industry offers awards. And you can also seek them out via that gizmo called the internet.

Once you have identified relevant awards, create a schedule with the deadlines, requirements, and budgets. (Alas, one must typically pay to enter.) Take on a few awards to get started, and soon your e-mail signature will be overflowing with accolades.

Conclusion
The Ever-Changing World of ORM

The future of online reputation management remains largely unknown and definitely a story that will continue to be written. At the moment, there are major forces competing against each other on a number of fronts. The tectonic plates of the internet are slowly shifting.

On one hand you have the undeniable fact that people will continue to make mistakes, be associated with problems, and be victimized. My father, who spent 50 years as a corporate attorney and counseled people dealing with all kinds of professional and personal business matters, wisely told me that there will never be a shortage of people having problems and difficulties. It's a primal thing. We are all flawed in some way, and we all make mistakes.

And there's no reason to believe that these problems will not continue to end up online. As a species, we have evolved into active recorders of information: Neanderthals painted on cave walls, Gutenberg enabled mass production of the printed word, and today anyone can publish information globally via the internet. Unlike any time in history, we can quickly and easily publish or broadcast our own words, images, and video. Bolstering this, particularly in the United States, we have our constitutional right to freedom of speech and freedom of expression, and the bedrock of our nation also protects those who choose to say negative and mean things.

From a business perspective, companies with the most control over online perception are businesses whose goal it is to make money for their shareholders. While Google and other search engines are generally good corporate citizens with appropriate intentions, they have little incentive to invest their money and manpower to handle the millions of removal requests they receive each day.

From a technology standpoint, I have seen that some of the classic suppression tactics are not as effective as they once were. Just as Google continually adjusts its algorithms so it can't be gamed by search engine optimization tricks, so does it appear, according to insiders I know, less susceptible to attempts to bury or push down negative content.

On the flipside, there are movements to try to minimize some of the online unpleasantness. Google made it easier for victims of revenge porn to fight back, and the right to be forgotten in Europe offers an option not available elsewhere.

And some people in high places believe that one mistake should not follow a person for the rest of their online lives. Local, state, and federal governments are trying (some successfully and others not) to prevent things like mugshot photo proliferation and create more substantial penalties and punishments for cyber-misdeeds like revenge porn. Many private businesses, which don't view themselves as news organizations, are now more likely to respond and comply with requests to remove negative information, or at least remove it from search results.

All of these points are creating what seems to me to be a collective sense that pushing, promoting, and purveying online hate is not good for the collective internet. I believe that over time this growing sense of fairness will continue to gain footholds, and it will therefore be easier to manage some online problems down the road.

But for the foreseeable future, there will still be victims of online issues. People will continue to not like what they see online and want to do something about it.

Notes

Chapter 1

1. "2 Billion Consumers Worldwide to Get Smart(phones) by 2016," *Emarketer*, December 11, 2014, *www .emarketer.com/Article/2-Billion-Consumers-Worldwide-Smartphones-by-2016/1011694.*

2. "Eyes On You: How Many Times Are You Caught On Surveillance Cameras Per Day?" *CrimeFeed*, February 17, 2015, http://crimefeed.com/2015/02/ eyes-many-times-caught-surveillance-cameras-per-day/.

3. Bart Jansen, "FAA: Drone Registration Eclipses That of Regular Planes," *USA Today*, February 6, 2016, *www.usatoday.com/story/news/2016/02/08/faa-drone-registration-eclipses-regular-planes/80002730/*.

4. "Number of Employers Passing on Applicants Due to Social Media Posts Continues to Rise, According to New CareerBuilder Survey," *CareerBuilder*, June 26, 2014, *www.careerbuilder.com/share/aboutus/pressreleasesdetail.aspx?sd=6%2F26%2F2014&id=pr829&ed=12%2F31%2F2014*.

5. Lee Rainie, Sara Kiesler, Ruogu Kang, and Mary Madden, "Anonymity, Privacy, and Security Online," *Pew Research Center*, September 5, 2013, *www.pewinternet.org/2013/09/05/anonymity-privacy-and-security-online/*.

6. Elie Bursztein, "19% of users use their browser private mode," *Elie*, May 2012, *www.elie.net/blog/privacy/19-of-users-use-their-browser-private-mode*.

Chapter 2

1. "Blood Alcohol Concentration (BAC)," *In the Know Zone*, accessed May 11, 2016, *www.intheknowzone.com/substance-abuse-topics/binge-drinking/blood-alcohol-concentration.html*.

2. Monica Anderson and Andrew Perrin, "15% of Americans don't use the internet. Who are they?" *Pew Research Center*, July 28, 2015, *www.pewresearch.org/fact-tank/2015/07/28/15-of-americans-dont-use-the-internet-who-are-they/*.

3. Sandals Resorts Intl. Ltd. v Google Inc. 2011 NY Slip Op 04179 Decided on May 19, 2011 Appellate Division,

First Department Saxe, J., J. Published by New York State Law Reporting Bureau pursuant to Judiciary Law § 431.

4. Barry Schwartz, "A New Click Through Rate Study For Google Organic Results," *Marketing Land*, October 1, 2014, *http://marketingland.com/new-click-rate-study-google-organic-results-102149*.

Chapter 3

1. "Despite Higher Risks, Greater Percentage of Employees Are Holiday Shopping at Work, Finds Annual CareerBuilder Survey," *CareerBuilder*, November 24, 2015, *www.careerbuilder.com/share/aboutus/pressreleasesdetail.aspx?id=pr923&sd=11/24/2015&ed=11/24/2015*.

2. "Ex-CFO who slammed Chick-fil-A now on foodstamps," *USA Today*, March 29, 2015, *www.usatoday.com/story/money/2015/03/29/adam-smith-chick-fil-a-video-memoir/70629290/*.

3. "10 Brands Damaged by Social Media Disasters," *ZDNet*, October 10, 2013, *www.zdnet.com/pictures/10-brands-damaged-by-social-media-disasters/2/*.

4. "Honda Struggles With Negative Reactions to Crosstour," *U.S. News & World Report*, September 4, 2009, *http://usnews.rankingsandreviews.com/cars-trucks/daily-news/090904-Honda-Struggles-With-Negative-Reactions-to-Crosstour/*.

5. Rachel Emma Silverman, "Facebook and Twitter Postings Cost CFO His Job, *The Wall Street Journal*, May 14, 2012, *www.wsj.com/articles/SB10001424052702303505504577404542168061590*.

6. David Cohen, "Netflix CEO Reed Hastings Faces SEC Scrutiny Over Facebook Post," *AdWeek*, December 7, 2012, *www.adweek.com/socialtimes/reed-hastings-sec/409503*.

7. Eli Langer, "Oops! Twitter's CFO misfires with a private tweet," *CNBC*, November 24, 2014, *www.cnbc.com/2014/11/24/oops-twitters-cfo-misfires-with-a-private-tweet.html*.

8. Adam Tanner, "Love It Or Hate It, Ripoff Report Is In Expansion Mode," *Forbes*, May 9, 2013, *www.forbes.com/sites/adamtanner/2013/05/09/love-it-or-hate-it-ripoffreport-is-in-expansion-mode/#57217eff33dd*.

9. Bill O'Reilly, "The Worst Websites in America," *Fox News*, May 20, 2014.

10. Eric Pudalov,"What Are Some Cool Deep Internet Websites?" *Quora*, accessed May 11, 2016, *www.quora.com/What-are-some-cool-deep-Internet-websites*.

11. Brian Prince, "Target Data Breach Tally Hits $162 Million in Net Costs," *SecurityWeek*, February 26, 2015, *www.securityweek.com/target-data-breach-tally-hits-162-million-net-costs*.

12. "How Much Did The Target, Home Depot Breaches Really Cost?" *Pymnts*, February 26, 2015, *www.pymnts.com/news/2015/target-home-depot-reveal-full-breach-costs/*.

Chapter 4

1. The Power of Reviews," *Power Reviews*, accessed March 30, 2016, *www.powerreviews.com*.

2. Dr. Ulrike Gretzel, Role & Impact of Online Travel Reviews, Laboratory for Intelligent Systems in TourismTexas A&M University, in conjunction with

TripAdvisor, available at *www.academia.edu/4227473/ Online_travel_review_study_role_and_impact_of_online.*

3. Serena Dai, "Iron Horse Owner Shoots Back at Yelper: 'You Are Terrible at Finding Bars,'" *New York Eater,* January 20, 2016, *http://ny.eater.com/2016/1/20/ 10799392/iron-horse-yelp.*

4. "HBS Study Finds Positive Yelp Reviews Boost Business," *Harvard Magazine,* October 5, 2011, *http:// harvardmagazine.com/2011/10/hbs-study-finds-positive- yelp-reviews-lead-to-increased-business.*

5. Joann Pan, "Positive Yelp Ratings Can Boost a Restaurant's Nightly Reservations by 19%," *Mashable,* September 3, 2012, *http://mashable.com/2012/09/03/ yelp-ratings-study/#MMn8SJ8085qO.*

6. "Content Guidelines," *Yelp,* accessed May 11, 2016, *www.yelp.com/guidelines.*

7. "Don't Ask for Reviews," *Yelp,* accessed May 11, 2016, *https://biz.yelp.com/support/review_solicitation.*

8. "Report Review," *Yelp,* accessed May 11, 2016, http:// *www.yelp.com.*

9. "Report Review – It contains false information," *Yelp,* accessed May 11, 2016, *www.yelp.com.*

10. "Fact Sheet," *TripAdvisor,* accessed May 11, 2016, *www .tripadvisor.com/PressCenter-c4-Fact_Sheet.html.*

11. "Our Guidelines for Traveler Reviews," *TripAdvisor,* accessed March 16, 2016, *www.tripadvisorsupport.com/ hc/en-usarticles/200614797-Our-guidelines-for-traveler- reviews.*

12. "Problem with This Review," *TripAdvisor,* accessed May 11, 2016, *www.tripadvisor.com.*

13. "How Does This Review Violate Our Guidelines?" *TripAdvisor*, accessed May 11, 2016, *www.tripadvisor.com*.

14. "Why Is This Review Suspicious," *TripAdvisor*, accessed May 11, 2016, *www.tripadvisor.com*.

15. "Billionaire's Advice for New College Grads," *Forbes*, accessed May 11, 2016, *www.forbes.com/pictures/fljl45lkm/ted-turner-work-like-hell-and-advertise/#63068017a48f*.

Chapter 5

1. Lebron James (as told to Lee Jenkins), "I'm Coming Home," *Sports Illustrated*, July 11, 2014, *www.si.com/nba/2014/07/11/lebron-james-cleveland-cavaliers*.

2. Chip Bergh, "The Dirty Jeans Manifesto." *LinkedIn*, July 14, 2014, *www.linkedin.com/pulse/20140714180558-14928043-the-dirty-jeans-manifesto*.

3. Claire Cain Miller, "Why BuzzFeed Is Trying to Shift Its Strategy," *The New York Times*, August 12, 2014, *www.nytimes.com/2014/08/13/upshot/why-buzzfeed-is-trying-to-shift-its-strategy.html?_r=0*.

4. "Wikipedia: Notability," *Wikipedia*, accessed May 11, 2016, *https://en.wikipedia.org/wiki/Wikipedia:Notability*.

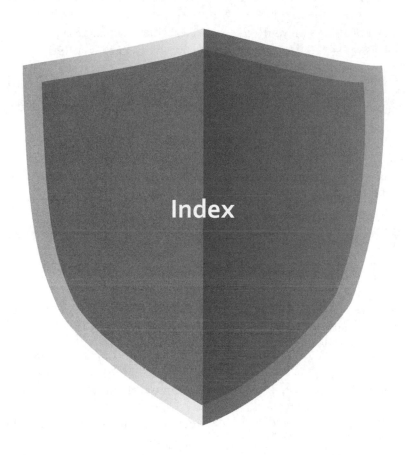

Index

About the Author

For more than 25 years, John P. David has counseled businesses and executives on strategic communications and marketing issues, from simple publicity campaigns to how to extract a company from the clutches of a $100 million Ponzi scheme. Yet, his most fascinating engagements have involved clients facing online attacks and other challenges. His strategic communications firm, David PR Group, counsels clients on marketing, reputation management, and public relations, and his award-winning insights are regularly published on the *Huffington Post*. Mr. David frequently speaks about online reputation issues to professional groups, students, and CEOs. He earned a bachelor's degree in public relations from the University of Florida and lives in Pinecrest, Florida, with his wife and two children. He can be reached via his website, DavidPR.com, for information on speaking and consulting engagements, and you can follow him on Twitter @JohnPDavid.